HUMAN RIGHTS AND INHUMAN WRONGS

HUMAN RIGHTS AND INHUMAN WRONGS

Sankar Sen, I.P.S. (Retd.)

GYAN

Human Rights and Inhuman Wrongs

Rs. 540

ISBN: 978-81-212-1087-4

Published in 2010 in India by
Gyan Publishing House
23, Main Ansari Road, Darya Ganj
New Delhi-110002
Phones : 23282060, 23261060
Fax : 011-23285914
E-mail: books@gyanbooks.com
Website: www.gyanbooks.com

Lasser Type Setting by: Rudra Computer Graphics, Delhi
Printed at : Chawla Offset Printers, Delhi

Contents

Introduction

The book is a collection of articles published during the last seven years in different national newspaper and journals. They cover various issues concerning law enforcement, terrorism, good governance, criminal justice administration and human rights.

The common thread running through many of these articles is the crisis in law enforcement and good governance in our country and the problems it entails for the law enforcement officers. Today terrorism in its various manifestations poses the most somber challenge before the country. Indeed the spectre of terrorism is haunting the world and India remains one of the worst victims of terrorist violence. Terrorist carnage in Mumbai on 26/11 is a game changer. It exposed in a blinding flash the fault lines of our security management and apparatus and underscored the prime need to strengthen the police, upgrade its skill and training and to depoliticize it. It seems that more acts of Maoist and Jihadi violence are going to rock the country and we are inadequately prepared to ride out the gathering storm. Structural reforms in the police to insulate it from extraneous pulls and pressures brook no delay, but there is lack of political will to implement them.

Articles on community policing and human rights seek to emphasize the oft-ignored point that without public support and co-operation policing a perplexed democratic society will be a herculean task. The police service has in recent times come under mounting pressure from different stakeholders and also an increasingly demanding public. Bureaucratic systems like the police are designed to be stable. But today systems that are unable to change are doomed to failure. Hope law enforcement officers and human rights activists will find this compilation of some use.

1

Aftermath of London Bombings

Terror bombings in July during early 21st century, fortunately did not kill anybody because the bombs did not explode. It could be seen that the bombers on July 21st, did not pick on very promising targets. The bomb planted in a bus, was virtually empty. However, the bombers have sent a chilling message, that bombings and mayhems are going to become a part of Britain's life for many years.

London police have launched a massive manhunt for the terrorists and their masterminds. It is estimated that nearly 1000 police officers often working 12 hours a day and 7 days a week, have been deployed. Some have been withdrawn from important criminal investigations and operations. It is estimated that cost of investigation into the attacks of July 7 and 21 is running into £5,00,000 a day.

During their operation, police marksmen gunned down one Charles-De-Menzes, a young 27-year electrician from Brazil. He was suspected to be a suicide bomber and shot down by plainclothes men, who fired 8 rounds from close range and aimed at his head. The police are now acting under new shooting procedures designed to stop a suicide bomber before he can detonate his charge. Shootings by the police are rare in Britain, as most of the British police officers do not keep firearms and this is now going to change. Normal guidelines for the police at the time of opening fire is that, they shoot for incapacitating the threat and that is why police normally target legs and other parts of the body and not the head. But now for incapacitating someone, who may turn out to be a suicide bomber, instruction of the police is to shoot at the head. The suicide bombers' brain has to be destroyed "*instantly and utterly*". There is always the danger, as has happened in this case, that the police may make mistakes in taking on the spot decisions. In the instant case, Menzes was wearing a warm coat in a hot day. Fearing that he might have a bomb beneath his coat, the police opened fire. The Independent Police Complaints Commission of United Kingdom has decided to enquire into the shooting of Menzes and find out if the police procedures are correct and some officers are to be held accountable. However, there is overwhelming public support for the police and their tactics. A You-Gov poll for the Economist shows that the people appreciate the work of the police and support this shoot to kill policy. Challenging a suicide bomber to stop may act as an invitation to trigger the bomb, so the police has to shoot first. People are also strongly in favour of tighter policing.

Police have arrested 4 suspects in the failed bombings of July 21, 2005. Police investigation is moving with speed, but lots of loose ends remain. Even now, investigators do not have a clear understanding of the twin terrorists plots. The police have not so far found any forensic link between July 7 and July 21 bombers, no phone calls or documents or other evidence to tie the two groups together. Further, says a British official, that bombs used on July 7 and July 21, come from different batches of homemade explosives. This means that either the same chemist has made from different batches or more than one chemist is involved. According to counter-terrorism experts of Britain and USA, the two attacks may have been planned, independently of each other. One of the bombers arrested in Italy, Osman Hussain, told the Italian investigators that July 21st gang had nothing to do with July 7 cell. This raises the frightening prospect of multiple jihadi cells, operating on their own. Investigators are also turning their attention to the support networks of these men and unless these networks are dismantled, the fear of further terrorist attacks remain very high.

The bombings also had their impact on life in London. If the objective of the terrorists was to spread fear, they have largely succeeded in doing so. A poll for the "Economist" shows that 90% of the respondents fear, that the city will be targeted again and 59% feel that, travelling in the capital is becoming increasingly hazardous. A possibility of a third wave of attack remains high and this estimate is based on concrete evidence, intercepted messages and interrogation of the suspects held outside Britain. It could be gathered during the interrogation of one of the suspects Osman that they simply wanted to make a political gesture against the Iraq war but the London police discounted this view and stressed that the second bomb attacks were also aimed at mass murder.

The bomb trail may lead to Pakistan. British investigators want to interrogate Nayeem Noor Khan, a Pakistani arrested in Karachi last year. He was Al-Qaeda's top communication man. His confession and other nuggets of information collected from his computer led to charges of conspiracy to commit murder and other terrorism offences against 8 men in Britain. British officials are also trying to interrogate Zeeshan Siddique, a British national arrested with false passport in Pakistan. He had confessed that he was party to a plot, to bomb pubs, restaurants and railway stations in Britain.

The bomb attacks were launched by homegrown militants and their process of self radicalisation has caused great concern to the police and other security agencies. The self-radicalized youth need not go to training camps but may turn to internet for bomb recipes and avoid the radar of security services. Sir Ian Blair, London's Police Chief, hopes that the Britain's Muslim community will rise and face this challenge and give no support to the terrorists. Britain now needs the support of Muslim community because, "*it is the community that defeats terrorist and not the police*". However, Muslim youths are feeling exasperated and alienated. There is an increase of hate crimes against Britain's Muslims. There were nearly 300 hate crimes reported within three weeks after July 7. Many were verbally abused and assaulted. There were also damages to mosques and other properties. Metropolitan Police Assistant Commissioner Tarique Gaffar has said that he had never seen so much anger among young Muslims. This has further exacerbated, with the increased use of stop and search and new shoot to kill to protect policy for dealing with suicide bombers.

Britain now contemplates draconian emergency laws to deal with the threat of terrorism. Indirect incitements to terrorism will also now be an offence. There is likelihood of radical Muslim preachers to be jailed or deported for their extremist propaganda. However, there is the danger that more disillusioned Muslim youths will be beguiled by the incendiary propaganda and illegal work of Imams banished by British bureaucracy. Britain is also considering setting up of special secret anti-terror courts to determine how long suspects could be detained without a charge in order to provide a way of meeting requests by the police and security services that detention before the charge should be extended from the current 14 days to three months. The new anti-terror package would include "*a new court procedure which would allow a pre-trial process*". Adoption of secret anti-terrorist courts will no doubt mark a serious departure from Britain's century-old adversarial justice system and will be a regrettable sacrifice of liberty to security.

2

Anti Dowry Provisions Remain More Unused Than Misused

Observations of Justice JD Kapoor of Delhi High Court that anti-dowry provisions of the Indian Penal Code (IPC) were being misused and such misuse are undermining the foundations of the institution of marriage and proving detrimental to the health of the society, has sparked off controversies. His observations have been decried by some women's organisations as "reflection of judiciary's male chauvinistic attitude". Justice Kapoor has also suggested that dowry offences should be made bailable as well as compoundable.

Though the stringent anti-dowry provisions of law, are at times misused, the hard fact remains that these provisions of law have remained more unused than misused. The Dowry Prohibition Act was passed as early as in 1961, to combat the cancerous evil of dowry system. The passing of the act, however, produced no tangible impact. Not a single case could be convicted in the entire country under the Act till the end of 1978. The Act defined dowry as 'property or valuable security given directly by one party to another as "consideration for marriage". As the

Act did not bar traditional giving of presents, it was difficult to prove that properties are given as 'consideration for marriage'. When the old Act proved ineffective, a new Act with more teeth was passed by the Parliament – Criminal Law (Amendment) Act 1983, to deal with the cancerious problem. It inserted a new section in the IPC, Section 498 A, to penalize the husband and relatives of the husband, if they treat a woman in a cruel manner, for which she is forced to commit suicide. A new section 113 A, was also inserted in the Indian Evidence Act, to enable the court to presume, that the woman has been tortured by the husband or relations of the husband to commit suicide, if she committed suicide within a period of 7 years. The burden of proof shifts from prosecution to the accused, a fundamental departure from the rules of Evidence Act. Further, the offence was made cognizable, giving police powers to directly investigate cases. A new amendment of 174 Criminal Procedure Code, made postmortem examination compulsory, where a women committed suicide in suspicious circumstance within 7 years of her marriage. However, even after the passing of the law, cases of dowry death and harassment pour in, from all parts of the country.

According to an estimate, more than 9500 women are killed every year in India over dowry. The period from 1990-2000 showed 18% increase in dowry deaths and 225% increase in cases of dowry harassment over that of the previous decade. In the year 2000, incidence of dowry death cases reported an increase of 4.4%, over that of the previous year. 31% of the cases at national level were reported by Uttar Pradesh alone, followed by Bihar 15.5%. However, these crime figures are suppressed figures, which do not reveal the real picture. There is massive burking as well as under reporting.

Society's response was further legislation. The Dowry Prohibition Amendment Act 1986, bans advertisement for dowry (Section 4A) and also enjoins on the state government to appoint Dowry Prohibition Officers (Section 8B). It was hoped that Dowry

Prohibition Officers, would render assistance to persons subjected to demand of dowry and help in collection of evidence and prosecution of the offenders. Unfortunately, Dowry prohibition officers are not functioning, in most of the states.

A study done by the Institute of Development and Communication, (IDC), Chandigarh, showed that for every reported case, almost 229 cases go unreported and unregistered.

Though 94% of the cases of cruelty by husband/relative u/s 498A, and dowry death under 304B IPC, are charge sheeted by the police; the conviction rates in cases of offences u/s 498A IPC are between 19 to 20% and u/s 304 B, 32%.

There is also considerable room for improving the quality of police investigation, in cases relating to dowry deaths. The Ministry of Home Affairs, Government of India, issued a circular containing instruction for handling of dowry death cases, namely, postmortem of the bodies in these cases, should be done by team of two doctors, disposal of bodies should not be permitted, without postmortem and every case should be investigated by an officer not below the rank of a Deputy Superintendent of Police. Photographs and fingerprints should be taken in all such cases. These instructions, have unfortunately, often been followed in breach.

It is also a fact that, very often, direct evidence is not available in cases of dowry death. In many of the cases, neighbours, who could have come forward to tender valuable evidence in the courts of law, do not want to get involved. Some members of the family, though sympathetic to the bride, do not give clear evidence in order to maintain prestige and honour of the family.

There is no doubt that provisions of 498A IPC and 113B of Evidence Act, have had a deterring effect. I know of cases, where the husband and the in-laws, have refrained from harassing brides, because of the fear of the stringent provisions of law. Unfortunately, mere existence of laws, will not prevent outrageous violation of human rights, like dowry offences. Laws do not protect human rights, only people do. During the debate in the Parliament on Dowry Prohibition Act, 1961, Pandit Jawarlal Nehru said "Legislation cannot by itself normally solve deep-rooted social problems. One has to approach them in other way too, but legislation is necessary and essential, so that it may give that push and have that educative factor, as well as the legal sanctions behind it, which help public opinion to be given a certain shape."

Nearly 100 years ago, Rabindra Nath Tagore wrote a moving story "Dena Paona" in which, the helpless heroine Neeru, was driven to death by cruel in-laws, because the dowry her father provided, was considered inadequate. It is a crowing pity that, the situation has not changed. The enactment of Hindu Succession Act, 1956, which provided for equal share in father's property to the daughters, to ask for partition of the dwelling house, appears to have unintentionally contributed to the evils of the dowry system. The prospective in-laws, instead of claming the share of the daughter-in-law, in her father's property after the marriage, prefer to demand the same in the form of dowry in the marriage.

Even the nature of dowry has undergone a change. No longer it is confined to clothes, utensils and jewelry. Very often the transaction is in lakhs of rupees with demands, ranging from investing money in business to building houses for the bridegroom. As the Director of National Police Academy, I had noted with distress, how young All India Services Officers shamelessly, asked for heavy dowry, throwing to the winds, all other considerations. Even educated women also silently suffer dowry torture and harassment. A survey conducted by the Centre of Social Research for the Ministry of Human Resources showed that, 90% of dowry victims covered by the study were educated – 30% graduates and 20% working women, who contributed to the family income.

Thus, there is no real redress unless educated women stand up and fight their battles. Ultimately, effective resistance has to come from the girls and their parents, not after they are abused but before. Brave girls like Nisha, Farzana and others have blazed a new trail. They have given a new fillip to the anti-dowry movement, which was almost petering out in the country. A resolute campaign is necessary, against this outrageous evil, to stir the conscience of the society and treat those, who are taking and giving dowry as social pariahs.

Memorable words of Mahatma Gandhi "acceptance of dowry is a disgrace for a young man, who accepts it, as well as dishonour for women folk" should ring in the ears of every unmarried young man or woman.

3

Child Sex Tourism and Paedophilia

Acquittal of Duncan Grant and Allan Waters in a paedophilic case, has upset many child rights activists, who are seeking to bring to the notice of the society, the severity of the problem of sexual abuse of children in India. These two men accused of paedophilia, were acquitted by Bombay High Court due to lack of evidence. They had been earlier convicted in 2006 by the sessions court. The sessions judge delivering the judgment, had expressed the hope, that it will serve as a warning to the paedophiles to stay away from India. The High Court, however, acquitted them and ruled that the evidence of the victims appeared improbable. The court also commented on the poor quality of police investigation. The Supreme Court on an appeal from a NGO, has now directed the Mumbai police, not to hand over the passports of the two Britons, till further orders.

Acquittal of paedophiles in a number of cases is disconcerting, as the sexual abuse of children both male and female, by the tourists has become a serious problem in the country. Unlike Sri Lanka and Thailand, this problem has not been seriously tackled or discussed. It has remained shrouded in secrecy, making likelihood of the child abusers, being caught and punished very low.

Sex tourists are often paedophiles, who seek out children to satisfy their sexual urges. Some of them are usually members of highly organized networks. They are also very cautious in their operations. Paedophiles shower attention on the children in the form of gifts and other presents. Most of the victimized children hail from poor families; children from hutments on the beach, children of migrant labourers, left unattended by their families. Paedophiles also gain children's silence, by portraying the abuse as education or as a game or by use of threats or violence, thus forcing them not to divulge their "*special secrets.*"

The phenomenon of the child sex tourism, has grown in size and volume, because of a feeling among the foreign tourists that the chances of detection are slender in the third world countries. There is also a belief that, sex with children is safe, because they are less likely to have contracted STDs. Further, the governments of many developing countries, with a view to encouraging tourism, tend to turn a blind eye to this problem.

Modus Operandi

Running an orphanage is often a typical cover for many paedophiles. Posing as good Samaritans, they set up orphanages where, young children are given shelter and later on sexually abused. In a well known case in Tamil Nadu, Will Heum, a Dutch national, setup an orphanage called "*Little Home*" in Kanchipuram District of Tamil Nadu. A number of small children, both boys and girls were housed in this orphanage. Heum used to drug these children and then subject them to sexual abuse. His vicious operations came to light, when one of the children escaped and filed complaint before the police. During investigation, it transpired that the Heum also entertained a large number of foreign tourists at orphanage and allowed them to sexually abuse the children.

Sometimes, paedophiles also pose themselves as producers of films and documentaries. The Mumbai police on a tip-off from an NGO, arrested a Swiss couple, who were picking up boys and girls from streets and sexually abusing them and also filming their various sexual acts. Thc police found sexually explicit paedophilic materials on the couple's laptop. The materials indicated that the accused routinely visited other Asian countries as well. The Swiss couple were convicted in 2003 but they left the country while their appeal was still with the Supreme Court.

Child Pornography

It may be seen that child pornography and sex tourism are closely interlinked. Sex tourists are often closely involved in the production of pornographic materials, in the form of pictures, and films depicting nude children and sex with children. Trafficking of pornographic materials, has become easier with the advent of internet technology. Hardened child sexual exploiters are often found to be producing, collecting and circulating child pornography. Aggressive paedophiles, according to FBI expert Kenneth Lanning, "*almost always collect child pornography*". They are also adepts in identifying vulnerable children from broken homes.

In India, Goa has become new Asian hub for child sex tourism. According to Child Welfare Groups, cases against the paedophiles go unreported and prosecutions are rare, despite strict child protection laws. The Goa Children Act, 2003, is an important piece of legislation, that has addressed the different issues of exploitation of children in an integrated manner. However, much depends on the manner, in which the Act is being enforced. The law enforcement in this regard does not inspire confidence. Children Rights in Goa (CRG), an anti-paedophilia group, has documented a string of cases, where the suspects jumped bail, escaped safe custody and intimidated the witnesses or acquitted due to lack of evidence.

Sex tourism in Goa became well known after the notorious case of Freddy Peats. He was looked upon as a respected man, who provided homes to young boys and girls. The shelter home of Peats, an Indian passport holder of Anglo-German decent, became a hotbed for European paedophiles. Investigation revealed that young boys were forced to unnatural activities, especially for the German tourists. The children were brainwashed to accept various sexual activities as natural. One of the victim stated that he was taken to Germany and kept there for six months. Peats was sentenced to life imprisonment and his conviction was upheld by the High Court. He died in April, 2005 at the age of 81.

Another study done by an NGO named *'Equations'* in 2002 regarding sex tourism in Eastern India revealed that the victimized children were mainly trafficked from places, in and around the tourist spots. In the tourist spot of Mamallapuram in Tamil Nadu, children were from nearby places and it was found that many of the children had to accompany the tourists, when they visited other states. The study also showed that, the majority of the children were from broken homes of families affected by poverty and debt bondage. Most of the children had no education and were procured by people, who are known or trusted by their families.

Qualitative research and anecdotal evidence suggest, that child sex tourism is spreading in different regions of the world. During the last few years, increasing number of sex offenders, particularly paedophiles, are shifting their operations from western industrialized countries to less developed countries, due to strict law enforcement and increasing vigilance in their home countries. Paedophilia is a worldwide racket, which police forces all over the world, are trying hard to contain. Known convicted paedophiles are listed, their movements are checked, websites monitored and so on. In India, the same rigour is missing. There are no stringent laws against child abusers in India. Beaches of Goa and Kovalam in Kerala, are becoming main destinations of sex tourists, seeking child prostitutes. A comprehensive policy for dealing with the problem has to be worked out with provisions for rehabilitations of the victims.

4

Crimes Against Elderly Persons

Demographic ageing, a global phenomenon, has also reached Indian shores. People are living longer and the graying population of the country is increasing. Today, in India 70 million people are above 60 and this number is going to be 177 million by 2025. One of the many problems faced by the elders, particularly, in urban areas, is the fear of crime.

The year 2004 was a fatal year for the elderly in Delhi. There were 11 cases of gruesome murder of elderly people, both male and female, by the criminals. The sensational double murder of Lt General Seth and his wife created widespread panic and consternation in the capital. However, significant upward trend in respect of crimes against elderly victims is noticed, all over the country. It is a fact that the elderly do not always report their victimization to the police. Studies done by the criminologists in the west[1] show, that many older persons are reluctant to report crimes against themselves for fear of reprisals. Their fear leads to reluctance to go to the police and this further makes them especially vulnerable to revictimization. Research indicates that elderly victims endure greater fear for their safety than is evidenced by their actual victimization rates. (Brillon Y. (1987). Victimization and fear of crime among the elderly)

Various factors are responsible for this escalation of crime against the elderly. First is loneliness. Many old persons are forced to live alone. In the event of any attack or any crime against them, they do not get immediate help. Second is their dependence. Because of their incapacity to live on their own, they are forced to employ servants or domestic help, even without being able to verify their antecedents. Elderly persons are particularly reliant on others, to work in the house and this makes them vulnerable to attacks, by criminals and other forms of confidence tricks. There are a number of cases of domestic servants perpetrating crimes on their masters, particularly, in Delhi.

Further, because of failing health, they can be easily overpowered. Age magnifies the likelihood of victimization. Criminals also know that a younger person is likely to fight back but an old man remains an inviting target. Many elderly people try to solve the problem, by reducing exposure to potentially threatening situations. Because of crime, and fear of crime, they do not venture out and participate in community life and develop a fortress mentality.

Elderly people find the consequences of crime far more devastating than younger people, who have more years to overcome physical, mental and financial shocks of any loss. Broken limbs, as a result of encounter with the criminals or loss of savings to a con artist may diminish an older person's quality of life and make some of them, live their last years in fear and distress. The elderly persons also remain susceptible to frauds that can destroy them financially. The FBI operations in the USA revealed deliberate targeting of older persons by con artists. Many elderly people have insurance, pensions, proceeds from the sale of the house and other savings, that make them attractive financial targets for the criminals. Again, many elderly think that they are safe from crime, when they are secure in their own house. But the criminals use the telephone as a tool to scam people, of their savings with devastating consequences. Telemarketing fraud is believed to cost Americans $ 40 billion a year and older people are disproportionately targeted.

It is necessary to take elderly persons' fear of crime, much more seriously and find creative ways to improve the quality of their life. It is aptly said, that a society is judged by how well it protects its children at the dawn of their lives and the elderly in their twilight years. Neglect of elderly person's concerns including crime, contribute to their fear that they are being viewed as disposable and obsolete. The fear of crime visible in the eyes of elderly today "serves as a mirror of our own future."

It is necessary that elderly persons, should follow some security measures, like going out in a group, keeping a dog as a pet, keep vital telephone numbers ready, inform police and neighbours if they are suspicious of someone, insist on getting their domestic servants verified by the local police. Some of the don'ts are:

- Don't be a recluse; socialize with the neighbours;
- Not to make ostentatious display of cash and jewellery;
- Don't trust strangers and open doors to any unidentified persons;
- Don't ignore any suspicious incident.

Sometimes, law enforcement officers, who contact with older people, are young and have little experience of working with the elderly. In USA, some of the police departments have created specialised positions within their agencies – the law enforcement gerentologists. They deal with crime and abuse related problems of aged persons and the opportunity of older persons to contribute to the crime prevention programmes. By developing a rapport with the elderly, the officers pinpoint the problems that impact on that segment of the population and then recommend ways to minimize the risk of victimization. They also alert the senior citizens to ongoing scams being committed against the elderly (Law Enforcement Gerontologists. FBI, Bulletin, February 1994)

In Japan, the elderly have been singled out for special outreach for the police. Police officers regularly telephone elderly persons, who live alone, to check on their wellbeing. They observe "Silver Days", when police personnel stop at the homes of elderly people. Particular effort is being made, to bring them into crime prevention organisations.

Some of the initiatives by the police in India, deserve mention. The Mumbai Police, with the help of some NGOs like Dignity Foundation and Agni, has embarked upon programmes to prevent victimization of the senior citizens. Under the programme, officers visit the houses of senior citizens, staying in their jurisdiction on a regular basis. There is also an Alert Citizen Watch Scheme launched by Mumbai Police, encouraging the public to inform crimes against senior citizens and the hazards of crime to which they are exposed.

Delhi police also under the present dispensation, embarked upon innovative programmes to create a sense of security among senior citizens and involved young students for this work. Under this scheme, school children are motivated to visit the senior citizens on weekends to share their problems. The results so far have been encouraging. However, Delhi police's servant's verification scheme is going through a bad patch. Their attempts to get information from other states on servants, working in middle class localities of Delhi have drawn a blank. Again, the residents are also reluctant to get domestic help verified, as they fear that their servants will feel insulted and leave them. Perhaps community policing with emphasis on face to face contact within the community may offer the elderly, their only access to help. Elderly victims need police protection to savour the golden years that they so richly deserve.

Reference

1 Brillon Y. (1987). Victimization and fear of crime among the elderly

5

Police-Media Relationship

In the murder case of Arushi, the police of Noida have botched up the investigation. The police top brass have taken credit for investigation with the arrest of girl's father. According to Arushi's mother, her husband is innocent. It is not Noida police but police all over the country are making shoddy investigation of cases. It is outragous for the Noida police to declare a reward of Rs.20000 for the domestic help when the dead body of the servant was lying on the roof. There is no justification for the state level police officers to be poor in investigation of cases. Investigating officers are seldom imparted proper training to deal with shrewd criminals, who increasingly rely on science and technology for commission of crimes. Most of the police academics in the country are officers centric. SVP police academy conduct courses for officers of and above the rank of superintendent of police who seldom investigate crime. If low ranking officers got training in big laboratories with advanced facilities, they would have surely lifted blood soaked finger prints from Arushi's murder scene rather than announce Rs.20000 reward for tracing an already murdered domestic help. As long as the states are reluctant to invest training their police force in forensic science and investigation, the citizens will continue to suffer botched investigation and mounting public pressure in the aftermath of a serious crime will lead to wrong arrests and subsequent acquittals after trial.

Police-Media Relationship

Police investigation into the Arushi murder case at Noida continues to be extensively covered by the media. There are many comments and criticisms of the investigation conducted by police and CBI. It is not known when the truth will be unraveled. Meanwhile, the media continue to extensively cover the case with their own theories and conjectures.

Initial police investigation however, exposed not only professional incompetence of the police, but also ineptitude of the senior officers to properly interact with the media. Some of the comments and remarks of the senior police officers before the media were unwarranted and should never have been made. This brings to the fore the wider issue of police-media relationship which in India remains somewhat confrontational. A content analysis of Indian Papers and Journals as well as TV channels over a period of time will go to show that the media, both print and electronic, make, sometimes justifiably, negative and pejorative references to the work and conduct of the police and depict them as insensitive and lawless. The police, on the other hand, accuse the media of sensationalism and exaggeration. Another police charge is that many of the media representatives are not only unsympathetic but betray lack of understanding and objectivity while reporting law and order problems.

The relationship between the police and the media in a democratic society need not always be smooth. But despite friction and constructive tension, to use the words of well-known journalist, there should be between them a large measure of understanding and a healthy appreciation of each other's role. On a more fundamental level, the police officers have to bear in mind that a free and open media fulfill an essential role in a democracy. They are the bulwarks of a free society. It has been aptly said by a perceptive critic that though Athenian democracy could rely on word of mouth to create public awareness a large modern state depends on its press; and so freedom, and quality of press have become sure indicators of the freedom and quality of the state. Nor has the situation changed with the advent of television and radio.

Article 19 of the Indian Constitution guarantees freedom of speech and expression and the freedom of press comes under the freedom of expression. The first amendment of the US Constitution has laid down that "the Congress shall not make laws abridging the freedom of press".

The media is interested in the news, the misdemeanor of the policemen and stories of their derelictions of duty and outright misconduct make news. They draw public attention and indignation. "The defaulting policeman", to quote the words of the Royal Commission, like the defaulting parson or school teacher is news. The upshot is that unbecoming conduct of some black sheep tends to sully the image of the entire police service.

The need for a more candid open door police-media relationships based on understanding of each other's role and responsibilities cannot be overemphasized. The justifiable complaints of TV and press reporters against the police are that they are unnecessarily secretive about divulging information to the press. They strongly feel that information is unnecessarily withheld till it has lost all its news value. Media and particularly regional papers and mushrooming TV channels gather information from other sources of dubious credibility.

6

Guns, Crimes and Violence

The massacre at the Virginia State University on April 16, 2007, was perhaps the worst peacetime shooting in the history of United States. The demented psychopathic student Cho-Seung-Hui in cold-blood, killed and injured large number of teachers, students and others. Cho killed his victims with two guns – a Glock 9mm semi automatic pistol and another Walther P22. Both are deadly semi automatic weapons and can fire bullets very quickly. One Professor Liviu Librescu, a 76-year-old Holocaust survivor, blocked the door of his classroom to restrain and slow the advance of Cho. This provided time for his students to escape through the window, but the professor was killed by Cho's bullets. The massacre at Virginia highlights the curse of gun culture in America. Earlier in 1999 in Colinbine, 13 high school students were slaughtered by two of their classmates.

At present, it is estimated that there are about 240 millions guns in America and a third of them are handguns, which are easy to conceal. It is reported that in 2005, nearly 14000 killings were committed with guns to which, may be added 16000 suicides by firearms and 650 fatal accidents. In 2005, more than 400 children were also murdered by guns. It is said that *since the killing of Kennedy in 1963, more Americans died by American gun fire than perished on foreign fields, in the whole of the 20th century, (*Economist, April, 21-27, 2007).

In America, gun crimes, which were steadily falling throughout in 1990's, are again showing signs of going up. The Police Executive Research Forum, (PERF), a police think tank, reported that violent crimes including homicide, have been rising rapidly in USA since 2004. There has been a sharp escalation of gun crimes, in many cities of America during 2006.

The leaders of both the Democratic and Republican parties have remained discreetly silent over the issue of stricter gun controls. Senator Dianne Feinstein of California has lamented, that shootings like these happen, because of the unparalleled ease, with which people can procure weapons in the USA. But senior leaders of both the parties have been diplomatic. President George Bush feels that, this is not the appropriate time to start "*debate on gun control*". Democratic senators are also not in favour of "*rushing to judgement*". Earlier the Democrats had energetically pressed for gun control. In 1994, President Clinton approved the bill banning assault weapons (semi-automatics rifles, hand guns, etc). But many Democrats now feel that, they had to pay a heavy political price for banning assault weapons. They lost the House of Representatives in 1994, because of the ban on assault weapons and then the Presidency in 2004. Now before the Presidential election 2008, the Democrats are not willing to antagonize the south and the west by asking for gun controls. This is the reason why the Democrats have abandoned their gun control crusade and in several states the parties recruited gun enthusiasts as their candidates.

There is constant and unyielding opposition of National Rifles Association (NRA), to any curb on gun rights. NRA feels that without guns, the Americans will be defenceless not only against criminals but also against tyranny. William Branton, the former Police Chief of New York (known for his zero tolerance of crime slogan), is of the view, that politicians on both sides, have been captured by the vocal National Rifles Association. Perhaps, he has a point.

In 1994, President Clinton signed a limited ban on assault weapons, but George Bush's allowed this ban to lapse in 2004. Bush administration has also opened the debate on the Second Amendment, which enshrines the right to bear arms. On March 9, an Appealate court in Washington overturned the capital's long standing ban on hand guns, on the ground that it violates the second amendment. In a 2/1 decision, the judges rejected the district's claim that second amendment applies only to the militias. The rights protected in the Amendments *"are not limited to militia service"*. In 1939, the US Supreme Court had ruled in the United States vs Miller *"the amendment was adopted with the obvious purpose of the protecting the ability of states to organise militias and must be interpreted and applied with that end in view"*. But recently, individual rights view has been gathering support. The case may go to the conservative Supreme Court, which is likely to quash state and local efforts on gun control. Some states and cities in USA, have tough gun control laws but these are being undermined by neighbouring states with weak laws. Only a serious effort at federal level, will perhaps work. It is learned that Michael Bloomberg, the Mayor of New York, has been able to pull together a group of 180 Mayors, to fight for this. The success of this initiative, however, is doubtful.

It may be mentioned in this connection, that two democracies with low crime and murder rates, are Japan and UK. Both countries have strict control on firearms. In Japan, possession of firearms licences is a rare privilege and the total number of licensees will be barely a few thousand. In England also, the total number of lawfully owned weapons is limited. Most of the firearms are deposited in rifle and pistol clubs and individuals cannot take these outside. In short, there are few firearms available with individuals to carry along. According to

Chris Nuttal, former Director of Research and Statistics of British Home Office, the gun lobby's argument, that it is the people that killed, not the guns; is not valid. The very presence and availability of guns, escalates the risk of wounding or death in every case of crime, including fights in a pub or at home.

Indian Scenario

Unfortunately, at present too many persons in India possess licences for holding arms and for every licensed firearm, there are at least 4 or 5 unlicensed ones. According to a veteran police officer, who was once Director General of UP Police, there are more fire arms, both licensed and unlicensed ones, with private individuals in the *Moradabad* district, than in whole of United Kingdom or Japan. In many dacoity prone districts of Bihar and UP, the organised gangs of dacoits use weapons from the licensed holders, either by threatening them or by making payments of money to them. Again, the bulk of the ammunitions used in country made unlicensed weapons, come from the licenceholders as manufacture of ammunitions is a complicated job requiring instruments not easily available.

Now, before the elections in UP, guns are in great demand. *Kanpur* has become the North India's gun capital. With little industrialization in neighbouring areas, guns are also one of the few status symbols available to the locals. There are approximately 8 lakhs arms licence holders in Uttar Pradesh. According to state Home Ministry, more than 20,000 of them are in Kanpur.

Indian Arms Act, 1959, did not provide strict penalties for illicit possession of arms. The old Arms Act of 1878, was viewed as a law by foreign rulers to disarm a subject nation. The new act of 1959, gave arms freely to law-abiding citizens to save themselves, but the benefit have been reaped, largely by the bad characters. They have acquired sophisticated arms on a large scale.

The (Ammendment) Arms Act of 1983, embodies some of the recommendations of National Police Commission and lays down enhanced punishment as well as minimum punishment, for serious offences, with the object of necessary deterrence. But, mere amendment of the law, though helpful, will not be adequate to contain the problem, which has assumed alarming dimensions. The National Police Commission further suggested, that arms and ammunition should be kept at safe places to avoid their falling in the hands of unauthorised persons. Before issuing licence, it should be specifically ascertained, if the licence holder is in a position to keep them in safe custody.

Smuggling of arms from Pakistan, also poses a problem. In Pakistan, a large number of authorities can grant licences for possession of even automatic weapons. There is a thriving clandestine arms trade across the border. Many of these weapons are *Dera* made. Dera is a bordering town in the Western Punjab, where arms manufacturing is like a cottage industry.

There is also leakage of arms and ammunition from army stores, because of inadequate security arrangements and lack of accounting and supervision. Some years ago, in a case of theft of cannon shells, from an important army establishment, the officers of the Crime Branch of Orissa Police, found during investigation, that arrangements and procedures for accounting, storage and checking of arms and ammunition were, far from being adequate and satisfactory.

7

Nithari Killings and the Need for Police Reforms

Nithari serial killings have caused a sense of shock and revulsion all over the country. Everyday, more skeletons are tumbling out of the cupboards. Number of children and women abused and killed, as CBI investigators are now finding, will be far more than what has so far come to light. Conduct of the police has been appalling and the criticisms of police apathy and callousness are more than justified. However, Nithari killings raise some wider issues of police administration and investigation, which must not be lost sight of. Otherwise, similar scandalous outrages of graver or lesser dimension will go on erupting.

The problem of missing persons in our country has not so far been properly addressed. The path breaking research study of National Human Rights Commission, conducted by the Institute of Social Sciences has shown that in India, on an average nearly 45 thousand persons go on missing every year, and of these nearly 11 thousand remain untraced. This is just a tentative estimate because the data have been collected from police records. As is already known, (and now reinforced by

Nithari cases) that, many criminal cases are either not reported, and if reported not registered by the police. NHRC research has shown, with hard data that, every year the percentage of untraced persons continues to increase.

State police agencies have their own procedures for tracing missing persons. Wherever the case of a missing person is received, no formal FIR (First Information Report) is registered in the police station. Only a "*missing person*" entry is made in the police station dairy. The Station House Officer forwards the information to the Superintendent or Deputy Commissioner of Police, who in turn, forwards it to the office of the police chief. Local police officials publicise particulars of the missing persons in the media, by circulating the available identification details and photographs. More often than not, efforts to locate the missing persons are soon abandoned. There are no sustained follow-up efforts to trace and locate the missing persons. Sometimes "*hue and cry*" notices are sent out to locate the missing persons but they seldom yield results.

At Police headquarters information regarding missing persons is lodged with the "*Missing Persons Bureau*", a wing of the state CID. They, in turn, forward it to the National Crime Records Bureau, (NCRB) of the Government of India, which acts as a documentation centre, but plays no role in the tracing of missing persons. Missing persons' photographs are also published in the Criminal Intelligence Gazette (CIG), brought out by the State CID. Even publication of the CIG has become irregular in many states.

Thus, virtually under the existing arrangements no serious effort worth the name, is made at any level to trace the missing persons. This is a gaping loophole in the existing arrangements for crime prevention and control. NHRC's study has shown that many of these missing persons, particularly women and children, are trafficked for commercial sexual exploitation, forced labour and other forms of abuse. I recall with some measure of satisfaction, that when posted as DIG in a Range Headquarters in Orissa, I could help a father to trace his only missing son, because I detailed an officer exclusively for investigation. The child could be traced by the investigating officer in Mumbai, after a week. However, this is not possible in every case because of manpower constraints.

In USA, private non-profit organisations, like the National Centre for Missing and Exploited Children (NCMEC), provide free services to the families of kidnapped and sexually exploited children. It also serves as a clearinghouse of information about missing and exploited children. In India also, there are NGOs like Children India Foundation (CIF), National Centre for Missing Children (NCMC). They have hosted sites displaying the photos of missing persons and children, on whom the police is conducting investigation. However, there is no systematic coordination and cooperation between the police and NGOs, dedicated to the endeavour. Indeed, efforts to trace missing persons are ad hoc and slipshod. In consequence, a large number of persons, particularly women and children, remain untraced. Resources and time at the disposal of police agencies are totally inadequate to deal comprehensively with the growing magnitude of the problem. Further, the police have displayed utter lack of sensitivity in deploying even their limited resources to tackle the problem and displayed no concern for the plight of the victims. A National Centre for Missing and Exploited Children should be set up with functional links between the government and non-government agencies working across the country. It is not possible for police alone to bear the brunt of the problem.

Further, in all cases of missing persons, a zero FIR can be registered to enable the police to take up sustained investigation. However, there is reluctance on the part of the police to register complaints because, any upswing in crime figures is viewed as lack of efficiency and competent performance on the part of the field officers. They are under constant pressure from their senior officers and the latter from their political bosses, to ensure that crime figures do not show any disproportional increase. There is conspiracy of silence from top to bottom, when station house officers refuse to register the case and drive away the complainants. The performance of the ruling party in maintenance of law and order on the floor of the Assembly is judged on the basis of manipulated crime figures. This tyranny of statistics is working havoc. On a conservative estimate, registered crimes in India are not even one tenth of the actual incidence.

Victimisation surveys are done in many western countries to know the actual incidence of crime from the victims, because police statistics are viewed as unreliable. This, however, is never done in India because this may reveal the massive burking of crime, that goes on all over the country. In UP, the malaise has surfaced in an aggravated form because of constant political pressures on the police to keep crime figures under control. One retired DG of UP Police had formally complained to the NHRC, about the illegality of instruction issued by then Chief Minister to the police officers that crime figures must show decline and not increase. Thus, crime statistics are like a scene from Alice in Wonderland. The images of crime figures in UP in 1996 were less than those in 1905 (90 years back). How many of our newspaper reporters know or mention this? In such a scenario, the poor, voiceless people are the worst sufferers and Nithari killing is a tragic illustration of the outcome of this monstrous malpractice.

The UP government, after bitter public castigation and media criticisms, has decided, as reported in the press, to suspend two senior IPS officers - erstwhile superintendents of police of the district and dismiss some subordinate officers. While disciplinary action against the aberrant police officers is called for, the hard fact remains that this does not address the systemic malaise eating into the vitals of the police organisations.

Police brutality and highhandedness are not a recent phenomenon. Even as early as in 1850, Torture Commission, later on, the Police Commission (1902-03) and subsequently many other commissions highlighted, misconduct of Police Station officers and their lack of concern for the rights of the people and, particularly, of the poor and downtrodden. They have remained unaddressed because of structural infirmities in the police, which today function as the ruling party's police and not people's police.

Today, in all states with greater or lesser degrees, there is constant political interference in the transfer, posting and investigation of cases done by the police. In some states, the police will not register FIR, unless the party apparatchiks nod their approval. The prime concern of the police officers, therefore, is to keep the politicians in power happy and do their bidding. They have no time for helping the people in distress, particularly, if they are voiceless migrants.

Many experts and analysts, have emphasised the need for improving and humanising police training for attitudinal transformation. But training, though a very important input, cannot overcome the impact of the organisational culture. Very soon, police subculture prevails over principles and norms taught during training. The answer is to insulate the police from corroding extraneous pressures and influence. Hence, the abiding importance of structural police reforms recommended by the National Police Commission. Recently, the Supreme Court in the case of Prakash Singh has given directions to Central and State governments for police reforms with a view to ensuring police autonomy and accountability and freeing it from asphyxiating political control. There is determined resistance from state governments, irrespective of the colour of the ruling parties, to implement these reforms. There is need for greater public awareness and vigorous pressure to implement these reforms directed by the Supreme Court. Otherwise, tragic Nithari killings will remain, just another grim episode in the annals of country's mis-governance and lack of resolve to break the *noxious* police-politician nexus.

8

Police Accountability and Civilian Oversight

Accountability means answerability for the proper performance of the assigned role. It involves more than mere responsibility to discharge duties involved in a job but also includes the responsibility of doing so, in a manner to the satisfaction of the party, for whose benefit it is being discharged. In a democratic society, the police remain ultimately accountable to the people. It also has a proximate responsibility to the law of the land, which in a sense expresses the will of the people. Protection of the basic rights of the people and compliance with law are the twin pillars of good policing in a liberal democratic society. The relationship of police to law is, therefore, instrumental as well as professional. It is a tool in their hands, for initiating action against the law-breakers. It also lays down the parameters, within which the police have to function. However, mandate of the police to use force, to curb violence and disorder, raises the key question that the police themselves should not indulge in abuse of force.

Exercise of police powers must be subjected to checks and balances. These checks and balances, if they are to serve their intended function, must be reliable and effective in their nature and operation and must be presumed as such, by the members of the community.

In a democratic society, the police remain accountable to diverse mechanisms – courts, legislature, departmental authorities and also to the community. Totalitarian states are called police states, because the police remain answerable to one person or group of persons in power. It is fundamental to the democratic societies that police powers, including power to arrest and to use lethal and non-lethal force, must be closely regulated through the mechanisms of an independent judiciary. The powers are ultimately subject to civilian control through democratic institutions. Continuing challenge before liberal democratic societies is to create mechanisms for organising oversight that can curb or correct the occasional abuses of police powers.

Many police officers as well as police scholars like David Bayley are of the view that for curbing abuse of police power, internal organisational control is to be preferred to external processes. Bayley has stated in his book *Pattern of Policing - a Comparative International Analysis* that internal regulation can be more thorough, efficient and effective than external supervision. A determined police can hide many things from external supervision and make it haphazard and ineffective. However, experience of dealing with police misconduct in different parts of the world shows that the capacity of police to regulate itself is limited and it does not carry conviction with the people. Attempts all over the world, to combat police misconduct internally has, as *Fitzerald Commission of Enquiry into Police Misconduct* in the Australian state of Queensland pointed out, have not been very successful. There is lack of public confidence in the police forces ability to investigate complaints against its own members. Public demand for civilian oversight of the police has received a stimulus from the widely held perception that the police cannot police themselves.

Turning to the evolution of civilian oversight bodies in democratic countries, it is seen that 1980s represented a watershed with respect to the moral dimensions of policing. During those years, civilian review bodies were created in many democratic countries. In sum, police lost their monopoly in determining whether police officers were treating their citizens right. There are strong reasons in favour of civilian review of police complaints. First, complainants feel more comfortable and free to air grievances. Second, a non-police officer's perspective promotes fairness. Third, greater objectivity and thoroughness in the investigatory process, will lead to a higher number of substantiated complaints and more appropriate disciplinary action against the corrupt officers. Indeed, civilian review is critical to the legitimacy of the police. Its purpose is not simply to punish errant police officers but to demonstrate to the public that it functions as a responsible institution. It also must recommend systemic changes and reforms.

Civil oversight bodies, in order to be effective, should have an independent investigative capacity. If an independent investigation can be launched, from the moment a serious complaint is received, it would reassure citizens, who may otherwise feel that the police will try to cover up their own transgressions. In the investigative setup, there must not be only police officers or ex-police officers but also investigators with different backgrounds like lawyers, academicians, doctors, who cannot be charged with pro-police sympathies.

Police Opposition

Experience in different democratic countries of the world shows that police organisations have been invariably hostile to attempts to set up civilian oversight mechanisms. External scrutiny of any kind is deemed repugnant by police officers, who feel that such scrutiny undermines police morale and effectiveness. In western countries like Canada, Australia, Civilian Review Boards were criticised by many police unions as "*Kangaroo Courts*", in which the constitutional rights of the police officers under investigation were not observed. But police resistance to the civilian oversight is more emotional than rational. Indeed, police morale will improve, because proper and correct police action will be defended by the civilians. Further, despite anecdotal evidence, available research does not support the contention that civilian review has an adverse effect on police morale. Survey of the attitude of police officers in different American police establishments confirms that civilian review did not have any negative impact on police morale or enforcement practices. The present evidence does not support the criticism that external oversight bodies have impacted upon police morale.

It is a fact that functioning of many civilian review bodies, has not always satisfied the complainants. In a major study evaluating the work of Police Complaint Authority (PCA) in UK, Maguire & Corbett, 1991 has pointed out that the system failed to command public confidence, because in most of the cases allegations against the police remained unsubstantiated. This happens because obtaining evidence regarding malpractices of the police is difficult. Very often, such malpractice occurs within the police territory and there is "*blue code of silence*" among the police officers. The PCA, in its report, also has emphasised the point that even the most minor disciplinary charge against the police officer must be proved beyond reasonable doubt. This high standard of proof raises a problem when there is a conflict of evidence, between a complainant and a police officer with no corroboration from either side. By contrast, civil suits against the officer, where the standard of proof is based upon "*preponderance of probabilities*" is often more successful. Maguire study also shows that some of the complainants were making the first complaint against the police in their lives and felt that it is like "*walking up to a six foot man*". They expect some kind of redress and reassurance that steps will be taken to prevent recurrence of similar police misconduct.

In India, National Human Rights Commission (NHRC), set up under Protection of Human Rights Act, 1993 enquires into cases of abuse and misuse of authority, as well as violation of human rights by the police. Almost 70% of the complaints received by the Commission pertain to violation of human rights by the police. Similarly, States Human Rights Commissions set up under the same Act, are also flooded with complaints against the police.

NHRC's enquiries have exposed many instances of police malfeasance. The Commission has recommended action against the errant officers and compensation to the victims. It has also taken steps to ensure human rights training and sensitization programmes of the police personnel. NHRC has also suggested systemic reforms recommended by the National Police Commission to insulate the police from extraneous pressures and build up institutional mechanisms to depoliticise the police. However, NHRC's endeavours to "*police the police*" have only been partially successful. Initial awe and wholesome dread of the NHRC, is now giving way to a more cavalier attitude on the part of the police. Some political leaders have also gone out of their way to encourage and abet violation of human rights by the police. Many of the complainants have also expressed dissatisfaction at the slow pace of the disposal of the cases by the NHRC and the State Human Rights Commissions.

Now, the Soli Sorabjee Committee has drafted the model Police Act of 2006 (the bill is on the anvil of the Parliament). It has recommended creation of State level Accountability Commission, as well as district level accountability authorities to ensure police accountability. Many senior police leaders as well as state governments have frowned upon the creation of these mechanisms. Their objections do not stand the glare of scrutiny. The police leaders should draw lessons from international experience. The oversight mechanisms, if they function properly, will enhance police credibility, restore public confidence in police and also ensure fair play for the police officers.

9

Fake Encounters Are Symptoms of a Systemic Malaise

Gujarat Police again found itself in the thick of an unsavoury and deplorable controversy. Report submitted by the Criminal Investigation Department of Gujarat Police to the Supreme Court, uncovers the cold-blooded killing of three persons, namely Sohrabuddin Sheikh, his wife Kausar Bi and one Tulshiram Prajapati, an alleged informer of the police. The CID report says that Sohrabuddin, Kausar Bi and possibly Tulsiram Prajapati were intercepted from a bus, by the anti-terrorist wing of the Gujarat Police (ATS) and subsequently killed. In this operation special task force (STF) of Rajasthan Police, was also involved.

The State CID staff had arrested three senior officers, namely DG Vanzara, RK Pandiyan and MND inesh of Rajasthan Police. Both Vanzara and Pandiyan have been placed under suspension. The police version that Sohrabuddin was a Laskar-e-Toiba operative and planning to launch an attack on the Chief Minister Narendra Modi, is an obvious afterthought. The fact however remains that Sohrabuddin had criminal antecedents and a number of criminal cases had been registered against him. He was not an innocent soul. The same is also true of Tulsiram Prajapati, another victim, who was probably operating as an informer of the police but had to be done away with, because he knew too much.

Fake encounters, staged by the police officers, resulting in the killing of even criminals is illegal and has very rightly landed the senior police officers in a sea of trouble. It is, however, a fact that false encounters are, at times, staged by police officers because there is pressure by the political masters to show quick results by means fair or foul. The public, particularly, the educated middle class, also do not mind if the police take the laws in their own hands and become executioners, particularly, with regard to the dreaded criminals. They love tough action against the criminals, who are escaping conviction and getting away scot-free because of malfunctioning of the criminal justice system. Police dilemma is compounded by the slow moving criminal justice system in the country. Trials drag on interminably for years and the outcome remains uncertain, particularly, in respect of criminals enjoying money and muscle power. Hence, the pressure on the police for short cut and extra legal methods. Very often, there is connivance of the political bosses and support of the public. This explains the reasons why the police officers,, who blinded the criminals in Bhagalpur, did not lose public support. The fact of the matter is that, encounters are not the problem, but the symptoms of a collapsing system of justice and shrill public demand of quick and extra legal solutions.

But the hard fact to be borne in mind is that encounters are counter-productive and encourage contempt for law within the police. The practice of policing to break law in the name of law enforcement is unacceptable and intolerable in a democratic society, governed by the rule of law. It is objectionable because it is arbitrary as a process and random in effect.

The National Police Commission, in its report, powerfully recommended that false encounters are to be sternly discouraged by the police leaders, as this is, not a remedy for the situation. The answer is to strengthen the law and legal processes. Unfortunately, some senior police leaders instead of resisting pressures emanating from the political masters very often bend backwards, to curry favour with them. I still recollect that as a senior officer in-charge of Criminal Investigation Department of Orissa police, I was berated by a Minister for not mastering "*all the tricks*" of police tradecraft. But by succumbing to illegal directions, the police officers may land themselves in deeper morass. And this precisely happened in the following case. Vanzara was the apple of the eye of the political masters and particularly, the Chief Minister. He earned kudos as an encounter specialist. He has now been dumped because the political establishment in Orissa, wants to present an untarnished image before the Supreme Court. Like Cardinal Wolsey, Vanzara will have to rue his unthinking and unquestioning loyalty to the king.

But blaming trigger-happy police officers alone will not suffice. To deal with the problems of fake encounters, some systemic changes are necessary. The National Human Rights Commission on receiving complaints of false encounters from Andhra Pradesh Civil Liberty Committee (APCLC), held public hearings in Hyderabad and recoded evidence. The Chairman of NHRC, in a letter to the Chief Ministers asked them to issue directions to all police stations, through the Directors General of Police on procedures to be followed, where death has been caused in encounters with the police. The Commission was of the view that the right of private defence should not be manipulated to justify fake encounters. In the procedure outlined by the NHRC, it was laid down that in the case of an encounter involving the police, immediate steps should be taken to investigate the case and to ascertain how the offence was committed and by whom. If the police officers belonging to the same police station are members of the encounter party, whose action resulted in deaths, such cases should be made over for investigation to some other independent investigating agency, such as the state CID. A Magisterial enquiry should also be ordered in such cases of death. The next-of-kin of the deceased much be associated in such an enquiry. No out-of-turn promotion and gallantry awards should be bestowed on the officers soon after the occurrence. Unfortunately, the procedure outlined by the Commission remains on paper and has not been acted upon by the state governments.

Encounter Specialists

In many state police forces, there are "*encounter specialists*", who become favourites of the political masters and police bosses. They, very often, turn into cold-blooded liquidationists and extortionists, who enrich themselves by dubious means. However, when the crunch comes, they are left to fend for themselves and their patrons unceremoniously dump them. This is the lesson that many police officers have not yet learned. Violating the rule of law is not sound law enforcement and is not desirable even from the limited police point of view. There are cases, where the encounter specialists help the gangsters, in their intra-gang warfare. Empirical research on organised crime in Mumbai, done by the Bureau of Police Research and Development reveals how Daud Ibrahim got several of his rivals eliminated through the agency of the police, by tipping them in advance. Police response in many of the cases was for elimination and not arrest.

Again, in every police outfit, there are some violence prone officers, who figure again and again in cases of misuse and abuse of force. Very little empirical research has been done in India regarding these violence-prone, aggressive officers. There should be no hesitation on the part of police leaders to discipline and weed out these black sheep. It has also been found that some police officers are more likely to resort to violence and excesses when there are others officers to provide physical and phychological reinforcement.

There is demand from many quarters, to transfer the case to the CBI. The Supreme Court in my opinion, has correctly directed the state CID to carry on the investigation. Already some upright officers of the CID have courageously and tenaciously uncovered many dark details of the case. There is no reason as to why they will not be able to carry it to a logical conclusion, particularly, when CID investigation is being closely monitored by the Supreme Court. During my incumbency as the Director General in the National Human Rights Commission (NHRC), I had seen that in many cases, lapses and misconduct of the police unearthed by the investigation team of the NHRC, were subsequently reconfirmed during state CID's investigation. IG CID of Gujarat Police, who is heading the investigation, will have to hand pick some upright and competent officers. The Supreme Court will have to maintain a strict watch to fend off extraneous pressures and interference.

Shocking police aberrations in Gujarat also underscore the importance of police reforms now directed by the Supreme Court. There should be institutions like State Security Commission to insulate the police from political pressures and oversee its functioning in an apolitical and non-partisan manner. There should also be State and District Police Complaint Authorities, headed by judges to enquire into serious complaints against the police. Most of the state governments are opposing Supreme Court's directives, as they do not want to dilute their unbridled control over the police. It is not surprising that Gujarat, Rajasthan are the two prominent states opposing tooth and nail structural reforms in the police directed by the Supreme Court.

10

Police Recruitment Scam

Large-scale irregularities and corruption in the recruitment of police constables have come to light in UP and exposed what was not unknown before that political interference and money power have begun to play an increasingly sordid role in the recruitment of subordinate police officers and constables. In UP, altogether 22000 policemen were recruited during the previous Samajwadi Party regime between the years 2004-06. Several irregularities have been detected in the probe conducted by the present government after it came to power. Irregularities in the recruitment include, waving of police verifications to recruit people with criminal records, forging examination papers, caste certificates, fudging scores and changing laid down procedures and criteria for selection of candidates.

Malpractice and unabashed corruption in the recruitment of constables, that has come to light in UP is deplorable and reflects very poorly on the functioning and leadership of the police force in the state. Constables constitute nearly 80% of the police force at the cutting edge of law enforcement. A constable has maximum visibility and interacts with the public all the time, in maintaining order. He has to be physically fit and mentally alert for proper order maintenance and crime prevention. Head constables and constables can no longer afford to function as mere automatons recruited to perform duties of a mechanical character. The Committee on Police Training 1973, (better known as Gore Committee) observed that, *"recruitment procedures should be so devised that they are free from political, personal or other corruptive influences. The need for objectivity in selection cannot be over emphasized."*

Certain prescribed selection procedures have been laid down in the police manuals and in government circular orders for recruitment of constables; but what actually happened in UP is shocking and scandalous. There was heavy political pressure to select candidates, whose lists had earlier been drawn up by persons, who were close to the political power centre. The list was prepared on caste and pecuniary considerations. According to reliable information, each candidate had to pay between Rupees 1 to 4 lakhs for an appointment. Many young boys were compelled to take heavy loans or mortgage their lands to pay bribes to the officials and politicians.

The selection boards at different centres were constituted in a partisan manner and comprised venal and obliging officers. List of candidates to be appointed, were sent to the senior police officers heading the selection panels at different centres. The willing officers bent backwards and disregarded all norms and rules, for selection of candidates favoured by the political bigwigs, by lowering qualifying physical standards, downgrading interview yardsticks and also allowing outsiders to write the answer papers. Mandatory police verification was given a go-by in many cases and in some recruitment centres, someone else, other than the candidates, had taken the examination. In the process, the means and methods of malpractices also have undergone changes. In UP, it is reported that a private firm was hired, to check the objective types of answer sheets. In several answer sheets, whitener was used to erase old answers.

Incidentally, similar modus operandi was recently detected, in selection of candidates of a para military organization of the central government.

Officers, who do not play the ball and refuse to toe the line, are humiliated and hounded. I know of the case of a DG of police in UP, who was humiliated and stripped of authority, because he declined to accommodate candidates, who were recommended by the political bigwigs. The officer could not stomach the humiliation and took premature retirement. In UP, a probe by a senior police officer, into the recruitment scandal has further exposed, that some girl candidates were sexually exploited before being selected. This is another sordid dimension of the scandal. This allegation has triggered controversies. The concerned senior officer has been ticked off, but it is reliably learnt that there is substance in what was alleged. A through probe into the recruitment malpractices will indeed open a can of worms.

The UP government has annulled the recruitment of about 17000 constables and placed under suspension 25 officers of the Indian Police Service, who headed different selection boards. FIRs under different sections of the Prevention of Corruption Act, have been registered against these suspended officers. For the first time, a state government has taken this kind of determined action. This is welcome. However, the motive should not be political revenge. It will also be incorrect and premature to plan arrest of the officers allegedly involved, before investigation against them is completed. It will only cause demoralization and cynicism in police ranks. The occasion should provide an opportunity to set things right and establish a palpably honest and fair recruitment procedure and rid it of political interference and manipulation. Mayawati government instead of just scoring political points, should try to institutionalize free and fair recruitment in police. Otherwise, 20,000 dismissed constables and a large number of angry officers in cahoots with disgruntled politicians in opposition will add chaos and confusion in UP's volatile politics.

Unfortunately, malpractice and corruption in the recruitment of police personnel, is becoming a pattern in many states. Sometime back in Orissa, the state Vigilance Bureau had to start criminal cases against a retired DG of police and a number of police officers of different ranks, after detecting corruption in the recruitment of the police staff. Indeed, corruption in recruitment in public services, is an endemic problem of a developing state, with growing unemployment and economic distress. But, the police entrusted with the job of law enforcement, elimination of corrupt practices in recruitment, is not only vital for the health of the force but also for the well being of the society. Police constables, who join the service by making heavy payments, will extort money from the people to make good the money, paid earlier and indulge in various malpractices. They will turn into veritable extortionists and sully the image of the force. This is what is precisely happening now. Criminals in uniform are crowding the force.

However, there are silver linings. Some of the states like Karnataka, Andhra Pradesh and Rajasthan have streamlined recruitment procedures, which are fair, transparent, and by and large, immune from outside pressures. Given the political will, there is no reason, as to why this is not possible in other states. The recruitment scandal also highlighted, the imperative need for police reform – need to insulate the police from extraneous pressures and selection of upright officers for important assignments. Otherwise, the prevalent system of malpractice and corruption in police recruitment will continue and sound a death knell for police integrity and discipline.

11

Victims of Her Own Success

Kiran Bedi's decision to quit the Indian Police Service, makes one sad. She took retirement, almost two years before her superannuation to devote herself, as she says, in academic pursuits and social causes. She feels that Indian Police Service, no longer gives her any further sense of satisfaction and fulfilment. I have known and seen Kiran as a police officer, for more than two decades. She is a trailblazer – the first woman to join the Indian Police Service. In the sixties, when we joined the Indian Police Service, the general belief was that the IPS was meant for tough and sturdy chaps, willing to face many a hazard and not for the weaklings. It requires both brains and brawns. Certainly, it was a "terra incognita" for young women. Kiran was the first to explode the myth, and like a battering ram, broke the wall of the male fortress. Later on, many women officers joined the Indian Police Service and enriched it in many ways. As the Director of the National Police Academy, I have seen how young women probationers could outshine and outperform their male counterparts not only in studies but also in outdoor games and exercises. Many of them blossomedafterwards as outstanding officers and added lustre to the service.

Kiran has always been dynamic and a go-getter. She raged and railed against stultifying rules and procedures and never hesitated to express her views publicly, which sometimes landed her in controversies. Some of the senior officers have felt disturbed and discomfited because of her outspoken comments. However, the fact remains that in every charge she held, she left things a little better than she found them. Instead of only complaining against the system, she tried to improve things and usher in innovative changes. Her work as the Inspector General of Tihar Prisons, has been truly outstanding. As the Director General of National Human Rights Commission I had to often visit the Tihar Prison complex. I had seen how she not only improved the physical infrastructure of the complex but also inspired and motivated the prison staff. One of the banes of the prison administration of the country is that the prison staff are for a variety of reasons, demoralized and dispirited and there is no pride in the profession, which is the key to excellence. Prison administration, thus, remains mired in attitudes and practices that are obsolete and antiquated. She was able to impart a new Promethean spark of life in the dry bones of Tihar prison administration. Indeed, everywhere she had worked, she had been able to enthuse the subordinates and display inspirational qualities of leadership.

Today, the Indian Police and Administrative service have become totally politicized. Politicians rule the roost and the officers crawl when they are asked to bend. Someone has aptly said that crawling is always the best and safest, as one cannot be knocked down from that horizontal position. Political masters are not comfortable with officers, who are not willing to do their bidding. Kiran is perhaps the only serving officer I know, who has come out loud and clear in support of police reforms; seeking to insulate the police from extraneous pressures and making it people's police and not the police of the ruling party.

However, like all mortals she also has her foibles. There is criticism that she is a publicity hound and too often addresses the press in violation of service conduct rules. In a democratic society, media has a mighty role in shaping and moulding public opinion. But too much glare of limelight can create problems for public servants.

As the Director General of Bureau of Police Research and Development (BPR&D), she made her presence felt and galvanized the organization. She has not followed the beaten track and took many new and bold initiatives, which will have far reaching impact on the organization. I wish, she had continued as the head of the BPR&D instead of quitting the service. BPR&D constitutes the think tank of the Indian Police. At this critical juncture, when the Indian Police is grappling with enormous challenges, BPR&D has a seminal role to play in planning, mapping and working strategic road maps for the Indian Police. Kiran should have remained at its helm at this time.

It is a crowning pity, that an outstanding officer like her, who has been a role model and inspired many young men and women to join the police service, is quitting with a sense of disillusionment. Sometimes, the decision to remain or quit the service rested with her. Sometimes, one should listen to the voice of the heart and take a decision according to one's own lights. Perhaps, a new phase of her career, with greater opportunities for serving the society will unfold. One wishes her best of luck. However, the Indian police will miss her.

12

Police Reforms – A Categorical Imperative

Mumbai carnage is a watershed in the country's troubled history of dealing with terrorism. It heralds the advent of catastrophic terrorism. The terrorists displayed skill, sophistication, ruthlessness and caused devastation on an unprecedented scale. At long last, the country has woken up to the dire threats it faces from global jihadi terrorism. The Indian Parliament, with a rare display of unity among the political parties, has now passed laws, creating National Investigating Agency (NIA) to investigate cases anywhere in the country, relating to terrorist violence. It has also passed Unlawful Activities (Prevention) Amendment Act 2008, which provides more teeth to the earlier Act. The Statement of Objects and Reasons, for the National Investigative Agency Act of 2008, clearly states that "*over the past several years, India has been the victim of large scale terrorism sponsored across the borders. The need for setting up an agency relating to terrorism and certain other acts, which have national ramifications has long been felt*". Several experts and committees including, the Administrative Reforms Commission, in their reports have also made recommendations for establishing such an agency. These measures are, though belated, necessary to combat the monster of terrorism. It does not require much clairvoyance to predict that serious terrorist violence will continue to rock the country with greater intensity in the coming days.

However, Federal Investigating Agency and stringent anti-terrorist laws will not be of much avail, unless there are competent and efficient police officers and men to man the NIA and vigorously investigate the terrorist crimes. Unfortunately, the hard fact is that the police all over the country, has become thoroughly unprofessional and politicized. Constant extraneous pressures and interference in the recruitment, transfer and posting of police officers and men, has worked havoc with its efficiency and professionalism. It has corroded the morale of the force.

Section 3 of the Police Act 1961 provides that "*superintendence of police throughout the general police district shall be exercised by the state government.*" This provision of the Act, has been utilized unabashedly by the state authorities to interfere in the day-to-day working of the police. There is constant interference in the posting, transfer, promotion and punishment of the officers. Upright officers are either marginalized or bullied into submission. The Superintendents of Police in the districts have very little say in the transfer and posting of officers in the police station. Sub Inspectors, in many police stations, pay regular money to MLAs, to continue in their posts. This has snapped the chain of command and control within the force. The rule of law in modern India, a perceptive American scholar David H. Bayley has put it, "*has been undermined by the rule of politics*". Supervision in the name of democracy has eroded the foundation upon which impartiality depends in the criminal justice system.

The maladies in the police are manifold. Recruitment of police officers and men in many states, has now become a scandal. A large number of men join the service, by paying hefty bribes. Irregularities in the recruitment, include waving of police verifications to recruit people with criminal records, forging examination papers, caste certificates and changing laid down procedures and criteria for selection of candidates. Political bosses in different states are involved in the sordid game. There are no visible efforts to set the things right. Police training institutions in most of the states are in a bad shape and have become dumping grounds of demoralized instructors, who impart to the trainees negative views and perceptions.

Interference in police system by the politicians encourages police personnel to believe that their advancement in service does not depend upon the merits of their professional performance and is secured by currying favour with politicians, who count. A study conducted some years back by the Indian Institute of Public Opinion, at the instance of Ministry of Home Affairs, regarding the image of police in India, revealed that the political interference is seen by the public as a major factor contributing to the poor image of the police. The people consider political interference in police as a greater evil than corruption. Political interference is more pronounced in rural than in urban areas.

The Prime Minister, in his address to the nation, after Mumbai massacre, rightly emphasized that police reforms have to be implemented without any further delay. He had in mind structural reforms in the police, recommended by the National Police Commission (known as Dharam Vira Commission). Some of its key recommendations include:

1. Insulating the investigation wing of the police from external political pressures, with a view to ensuring freedom in the operational functions of police administration;
2. To remove Damocles' sword of transfer, constantly dangling over the head of chiefs of police of states and assure them of a statutory tenure after proper and careful selection;

3. Constitution of a State Security Commission, to help the state government to effectively discharge its superintending responsibility under the framework of law.

The National Human Rights Commission in its report, while roundly castigating the police for violation of human rights, strongly endorsed the core recommendations of the NPC to insulate the police from extraneous pressures and influence. A former Union Home Minister, Indrajit Gupta, in a letter to all the Chief Ministers (April 3, 1997) clearly stated that "*deficiency in the functioning of the police in our country have arisen largely due to overdose of unhealthy and petty political interference at various levels*". He urged the Chief Ministers to introduce reforms recommended by the National Police Commission. All the Chief Ministers, including the Chief Minister of the state he belonged, to ignored the letter.

Now the Supreme Court, in a path breaking decision, in the case of Prakash Singh Vs Union of India, has given clear directives to the center and state governments to implement the core police reforms recommended by the National Police Commission to insulate the police from extraneous pressures and influence. The seven point directives of the Supreme Court include, a fixed tenure of the State Director General of Police, separation of investigation wing from law and order wing, setting up of a Police Establishment Board to decide on transfers, posting and service related matters of officers up to the rank of Deputy Superintendent of Police and setting up of new Security Commission in every state, so that state governments do not exercise unwarranted influence or pressure on the police. The independence of the Security Commission has sought to be ensured by the inclusion of the leader of the opposition, a retired or sitting High Court judge and some important non-political citizens. It will also act as a forum of appeal for disposal of representations of police officers of the rank of Superintendents of Police and above, if he is subjected to illegal or irregular orders in the performance of his duties.

However, the center and state governments are dragging their feet and trying to scuttle police reforms in various ways. As the existing arrangement ideally suits the political masters, there is stubborn rearguard action to circumvent it. However, it is hoped that in the present grim scenario, the police reforms will be implemented without any delay so that the country gets an apolitical, efficient and revamped police force to face the challenges from the forces of disruption and destabilization. It is necessary for the civil society to press the demand for an upright, efficient and depoliticized police force. There can be no further delay.

13

Complaints Against the Police-Investigatory Role of the National Human Rights Commission

The National Human Rights Commission (NHRC) was set up under the Protection of Human Rights Act, 1993 for the protection and promotion of human rights in India. One of the important functions of the Commission, as outlined in Section-12A of the Act, is to enquire into the violation of human rights and abetment thereof, by negligence in the prevention of such violation by a public servant. Since its inception, the NHRC had started receiving numerous complaints of violation of human rights from all over the country. A large number of such complaints concern violation of human rights by the police. The complaints registered in the NHRC during the year 2004-05 are (59,420), 2005-06 (74,442), 2006-07 (82,228), 2007-08 (1,00,616) and 2008-09 (90,950). Complaints of various sorts against the police and the security personnel, ranging from simple to odious, now constitute more than half of the total number of complaints being received at the commission. Some of the complaints against the police are frivolous, vexatious and often engineered by the criminal elements for discomfiting the police. Nevertheless, there are also many true cases of serious violation of human rights by the police, which include arbitrary arrest, implication in false cases, misconduct and misbehaviors towards women and custodial violence.

One of the important instructions, issued by the NHRC immediately after its constitution was that the death in police custody should be reported to it within 24 hours. The Commission's letter mentions that, failure to report such cases within 24 hours will lead to a presumption that the authorities are trying to suppress the facts. During the period from 1.4.95 to 31.3.96, 136 deaths in police custody were reported to the Commission. The figure shot up to 188 during the period from 1.4.96 to 31.3.97. From 1.4.97 to 31.3.98, 193 cases of deaths in police custody were reported. All cases of death in police custody, do not invariably mean torture or violence by the police. But in quite a few cases, deaths in police lockups due to torture and misuse of custody by the police have come to light.

In a number of serious offences of misuse of authority and commission of custodial crimes by the police, the NHRC first asked for reports from the State authorities. Finding that the reports were inadequate or revealed attempts to cover up the lapses of the police officers, it had to order investigation of the cases by its own staff. The Protection of Human Rights Act (HRC), section 11(1)(B) provides that the Commission will have its own investigative staff under an officer, not below the rank of the Director General of Police and such other officers and staff as may be necessary for the efficient performance of the functions of the Commission. I was its first Director General and remained incharge of the Investigating Wing of the National Human Rights Commission for more than four years.

In this connection, it may be mentioned that police officers in different countries of the world have never appreciated or approved investigation into cases of complaints against the police by an outside agency. They view it as some sort of interference in the internal management of the police. Even upright senior officers also feel that police misconduct can be controlled only through vigorous internal regulation. They are of the view that the senior officers have nose for bad apples, while having a sympathetic understanding of stresses and strains that cause police misconduct. Outsiders will fill on both counts and end up being both ineffective and unfair. There is also the danger that the police officers are likely to close ranks and try to screen the offenders from scrutiny by an outside agency. However, experience in different democratic countries of the world has shown that exclusive reliance on police regulation, is not sufficient to check misuse of police powers. It is the reason, why civilian oversight of the police has emerged as one of the legitimate means by which the State authorities try to ensure check on abuse or misuse of police powers.

It is normally very difficult to substantiate complaints against the police personnel. Very often, the malpractice occurs in the police territory and the officers, who break the laws have all the opportunities to hide their misdeeds. There is also the code of silence among the police officers. This is the reason why unsubstantiated complaints against the police should be considered as complaints that lack adequate evidence to support rather than unjustified complaints. Initially, senior police officers and their political masters viewed the NHRC as a police-bashing agency. In many meetings, senior police officers expressed their grievance that only the police had been singled out as the violator of human rights. It had to be painstakingly explained to them that the violation of human rights are committed by many other agencies of the government, but violation by the police are far more serious and sinister because they deprive the people of their rights to life and liberty and leave behind scars, which take long time to heal. Our efforts in the NHRC, from the beginning, was to carry the police leadership with us while enquiring into the complaints against the police and also to make clear that the object was not just to punish the officers but ensure compliance with rules and laws by the police. Willing compliance is always to be preferred to the exacted deterrence.

CASE OF ATAL BIHARI MISHRA

Whenever instances of serious misconduct by the police came to light during investigation by the NHRC officers, the Commission in many cases asked the State CID to undertake further investigation and report to the Commission. One such well known and important case, was the custodial death in Ballia (Uttar Pradesh) of one Atal Bihari Mishra, a student of Banaras Hindu University. The former Prime Minister, Chandrasekhar raised the matter in the Parliament and urged the government to refer the case to the NHRC. Initially, the district police tried to show that the death of Mishra was caused by a bomb attack by some hoodlums on the vehicle he was traveling in. Investigation by the Senior Superintendent of Police of the Commission revealed that Mishra was implicated in a false case and tortured to death in the police station because of political differences between his father and a local politician belonging to the then ruling party in UP.

At the instance of the Commission, the State CID took up the investigation and submitted a chargesheet against as many as 19 police officers, including, the Superintendent of Police. The Commission further directed the State government, to pay to the father of the deceased, a sum of Rs. 5 lakhs by way of interim compensation. It also urged the Government of UP to consider sympathetically, the prayer of the family for an appointment at an appropriate level, having regard to the eligibility and qualifications of a suitable member of the family on compassionate grounds. The Government of UP took the stand that as the case of Atal Bihari Mishra was pending in the court of Chief Judicial Magistrate, Ballia, compliance of the recommendations of the Commission could be possible, only after the police officials accused were found guilty of the charges.

The Commission considered the stand taken by the State government as incorrect and pointed out that the award of interim relief under Sub-Section 3 of Section 18 of the Protection of the Human Rights Act, 1993 is not dependent upon the establishment of the culpability of the public servant. The remedy is "independent of such pettifoggeries". The Commission pointed out, 'the meaning to be given to Section 18(3) by any state, professing to be a welfare state, should ensure a liberal construction to promote the philosophy of the statute and to advance its beneficent and benevolent purposes. The view that implies that administration of such, 'immediate interim relief' could only be at the end of the day, after the guilt of the offending public servant is established in a criminal trial on the standards of criminal evidence, would nullify the great humanism the statute seeks to enshrine. The Commission hopes that the Government of UP is only an ally of those values and will respond in a way, which accords with the message and philosophy of the law and its obligation as a welfare state'. The Government of UP, subsequently, paid the compensation to the victim's family as recommended by the Commission.

There was another unfortunate case of the death of one Usman Ansari of Nagpur, where the Commission had to intervene because senior police officials were trying to cover up the misdeeds of their subordinates. In this case, the Commission received a complaint from Smt Hamida Begam, a resident of Nagpur, alleging that her husband Usman Ansari was forcibly taken by four police constables from their home to prepare food for a party that was organized to celebrate the promotion of the Head Constable as Sub-Inspector. Next morning, the dead body of her husband was found on the road near the place, where the party was held.

In response to the Commission's notices, the Director General of Police, Maharashtra, informed the Commission that investigation of the case was closed by State CID as nobody could give definite clues, which would help to detect the culprits.

The Commission found the report of the State CID as unsatisfactory and directed its own investigation officers to enquire into the matter. The Investigation Division's report pointed out that investigation by the State CID was perfunctory and an attempt had been made to cover up the facts. The Commission's investigation further revealed that a scuffle had taken place between the deceased and some policemen, who had come to attend the party and the deceased had sustained an injury on the skull, which caused his death. Death was not caused because of the road accident. The Commission asked the Government of Maharashtra to get the matter investigated by the CBI and to pay a compensation of Rs 2 lakhs to the next of kin of the victim. The Commission directed that the amount so paid may be subsequently recovered from those police personnel, whose guilt will be established from an independent investigation.

Decisive investigation of the NHRC in a case of the killing of a businessman at Ranchi, had a salutary impact. The Commission received a complaint from one Reeta Dhawan of Ranchi that the Maruti van of her husband, while he was returning from Varanasi, was surrounded by six policemen near the Police Civil Lines, Ranchi. They demanded Rs. 1 lakh and on being refused, shot at the petitioner's husband and others from a point blank range and killed them. This happened on December 5, 1993. They also removed the gold chain, rings and wrist watch from the body of the deceased. At Commission's instance, a criminal case was started against the police officers, who were suspended. Officers were convicted in the case and sentenced to death. The Commission also directed that an immediate payment of Rs. 10 lakh should be awarded to Reeta Dhawan without prejudice to her private law rights for damages. The State government contended that the accused persons have already been convicted and sentenced to death, the government found no justification for paying compensation of Rs 10 lakh, as this will cause an unnecessary financial burden on the State. The Commission pointed out that stand of the government was incorrect. The establishment of culpability of public servants in a criminal trial and their conviction, does not put at rest, the caliming for compensation or immediate relief to the dependents of the victims as envisaged in the Section 18(3) of the Protection of Human Rights Act. The establishment of culpability of the involved public servants cannot absolve the State of its liability for compensation. The State government complied with the recommendations of making payment to Reeta Dhawan.

In another case concerning high-handedness of PAC personnel at Varanasi, the Commission took suo-motu cognizance of a newspaper report, which appeared in The Pioneer dated 5.8.1997 under the caption "Students face PAC jawans' wrath". In this case also, investigation done by the officers of the Investigation Division of the Commission established the high-handedness on the part of PAC personnel in confining and assaulting a group of students, who had gathered to felicitate a friend on his academic achievement. Later on, at the instance of the Commission, the State CID took up the investigation of the case and submitted a charge sheet against 28 PAC personnel for various offences under the Indian Penal Code in the court of the Chief Judicial Magistrate, Varanasi. Again, taking into account the unprovoked nature of the attack and wrongful confinement, the likely cost of medical treatment involved and the violation of the dignity and integrity of the person, the Commission recommended interim compensation by way of immediate relief as per Sub-Section 3 of Section 18 under the Protection of Human Rights Act, 1993. The compensation mount for each of the students ranged between Rs. 10,000 to Rs. 25,000. The Government of UP had confirmed that the sanction had been accorded by the Governor of UP for payment of immediate relief to the victims as directed by the Commission.

VIDEO-FILMING OF POST-MORTEM EXAMINATION

The NHRC also felt concerned at the uneven quality of post-mortem report. A number of instances came to the

Commission's notice, where post-mortem reports appeared to have been doctored due to the influence of the officials, who perpetrated the offence. There was also inordinate delay in writing of the post-mortem reports. In cases of custodial deaths, very often, the fate of cases depends upon the opinions given by the doctors in the post-mortem reports. There can be total miscarriage of justice, if the reports are manipulated and the doctors intimidated. The Commission, therefore, recommended "video-filming" of post-mortem examinations and sending of tapes to the Commission for scrutiny, with a view to preventing such malpractices. Twentytwo States and Union territories have now accepted the recommendations, while two others have stated that they were examining the matter. The Commission is pressing the remaining States, to accept its recommendations without any further delay. The Commission also circulated for adoption, a model autopsy form, that took into consideration the work done by the United Nations on the subject and special circumstances prevailing in the country. Seventeen States and Union territories have accepted the model autopsy form and the concomitant procedures recommended by the Commission.

VISITS TO THE POLICE LOCKUPS

Disturbed by increasing reports of violence in the police lockups, the Commission decided that its officers will make visits to the police lockups. Section 12C of the Protection of Human Rights Act provides that the Commission shall visit under intimation to the State government, any jail or institution under the control of the State government, where persons are detained or lodged for purposes of proper treatment, reformation or protection and also to study the living conditions of the inmates and make recommendations thereon. The Secretary-General of the Commission, wrote to the Chief Secretaries of the States, to issue necessary instruction to enable the officers of the NHRC to visit the State to undertake visits to police lockups as well. Twentysix States/Union territories have since accepted the suggestion. The Commission is pursuing this matter with the governments of Arunachal Pradesh, Assam, Jammu & Kashmir, Manipur and the Union territories of Daman and Diu, who are yet to respond positively. The Commission also issued detailed instruction to the officers of its Investigation Division regarding the manner, in which they are to inspect the lockups. A list of "dos and don'ts" has been prepared and circulated to the NHRC officers.

HUMAN RIGHTS CELLS

The Commission has also now urged the Police administration in the States to set up Human Rights Cells in the Police Headquarters, which will serve as the main link between the NHRC and the State police agencies. This Police Complaints Authority at State Police Headquarters, will function as an oversight body. It will also take steps to ensure human rights training and sensitization of the police officers and men, organize seminars and workshops on human rights in association with the State Human Rights Commissions and the NHRC, to actively promote human rights, literacy and awareness through different seminars and workshops.

The Commission has further strongly felt the need for systemic reforms in the police. It has emphasised the need for implementing speedily some of the important recommendations of the National Police Commission for insulating the police from external pressures and influence and for building up of some institutional mechanisms to depositaries the police. The Commission felt gratified when the then Home Minister, Indrajit Gupta, in a letter to Chief Ministers of States in 1997, chose to pursue the matter and fully endorsed the recommendations of the National Human Rights Commission and the National Police Commission for systemic reforms in police. The Commission also impleaded itself as a party, in the case of Prakash Singh vs. Union of India and others before the Supreme Court of India, which relates specifically to the implementation of the recommendations of the National Police Commission. In a comprehensive affidavit, the Commission highlighted the need for insulation of the police from extraneous pressures and other structural reforms, so that the police is not utilized by the party in power to subserve its own ends. The Commission looks forward to the verdict of the Supreme Court, which will have an important bearing on systemic police reforms and help the police to uphold law and protect human rights with greater competence.

14

Violence Prone Police Officer

In modern democratic societies, the police is vested with authority of using legitimate and situationally justified force against the citizens. Albert Reiss has aptly said that, *"at law, police in modern democracy posses a virtual monopoly of legitimate use of force against civilians and to examine the police use of force is to examine an activity at the core of politics and society."*

In India, very often there are justified and shocking complaints, about misuse or abuse of force by police. An impression prevails that the police forces in the country are full of bloodthirsty maniacs and sadists, who relish the sight of broken skulls and blinded eyes. In police force everywhere, there are always some officers and men, who are violence prone and trigger-happy, but there are also many others, who are idealistic, considerate and have empathy for the public. Unfortunately, regarding these aggressive trigger-happy Police officials and their motivation and characteristics, very little empirical research has been done in India.

In USA, Christopher Commission looked into the use of force by the Los Angeles Police (1991) after the Rodney King incident and pin pointed a group of officers, who are aggressive, violence prone and resort to improper use of force. The Commission identified, by going through the records of the Los Angeles Police Department (LAPD), that there were about fortyfour officers, with six or more allegations of excessive use of force or improper tactics, during the period from 1986-1990. The Christopher Commission, however, also pointed out that, higher number of cases of use of force by an officer may not always show that he is violence-prone. Active officers, assigned to high crime areas or officers on specialized duties will use force more often and generate more complaints against them than an ordinary officer, performing routine duties. The Commission also noted that there were many successful and productive officers in high crime areas, who do not accumulate many complaints against them.

Organizational Culture

According to many criminologists and police scholars, frequent use of force and violence by an officer is influenced by organizational style and culture. In police forces in India, as well as many other countries, officers are evaluated by number of arrests made, cases detected, charge sheets submitted and calls attended. They are appreciated for their "*hard-nosed policing*" and not for displaying concern for the public. This kind of assertive hard-nosed policing, goes to create a mentality that alienates police officials from the community. Again, in many police organizations, there is an "*ethic of masculinity*". This leads many officials to hanker after *man-of-action* image. A young police recruit, who does not manifest a man-of-action image, is not held in high esteem by his colleagues and very often not accessible to inner circles of the organization.

Peer Approval

It is also a known fact that in many police organizations, rough and ready use of force meets with peer approval. In order to gain peer approval, new officers seek out encounters, which can turn out to be violent and which have potential for conflict. Dispensing street justice, become an accepted style of working and a convenient rationale for these action oriented officers. It is also a fact that some of these officers become dispensers of street justice, because they have limited verbal or interpersonal skills, which they try to cover up by display of authority. They are also oversensitive to affronts. They equate disrespect as aspersions on their authority or masculinity. It is these officers, who lacking poise and confidence in themselves, become oversensitive to affronts and often act violently.

Scholars like Niederhoffer often have felt that many police officers, who constantly witness man's inhumanity to man, turn cynical. This cynicism has a corroding effect. Many of them become disoriented and display violent streaks in encounters with the citizens. In this connection, perhaps it will be good to make a distinction between brutality and unnecessary use of force. Brutality is wrongful and willful use of force by exceeding the bounds of the office, but unnecessary use of force occurs, when police officers, who could have easily tackled the situation by peaceful means, resort to use of force. Very often, young officers resort to unnecessary use of force, which could have been avoided by experienced and capable officers. It is this unnecessary and avoidable use of force that causes considerable friction between the police and community. Police brutality, on the other hand, often takes place out of public sight. The police also take precautions to see that their brutal deeds escape detection and public notice.

The report of Christopher Commission makes references to LAPD's assertive style of law enforcement as the main reason for aggressive confrontation with the public. It has traced this style of policing to a professional organizational culture, cultivated by LAPD through training and incentive structure. Officers in LAPD were rewarded for "*hard-nosed*" policing, which is likely to bring police in conflict situations with the citizens.

The Commission noted that the administration of Los Angeles Police Department failed to discourage improper use of force. Many complaints that were filed against the police personnel, could not be substantiated as a result of the flawed procedures for investigating the complaints. Further, sanctions imposed on the police officers, against whom charges of violence and improper use of force substantiated, had been light, failed both as a deterrent and as a message that such behaviour was inappropriate. The commission also concluded that Los Angeles police department's incentive structure influenced directly officers' behaviour and there was a link between formal administrative structure and informal organizational culture.

Some research on the use of deadly force has further shown that strict administrative control has a restraining effect on the frequency with which, officers use their firearms. Policies laying down clear rules regarding deadly use of force and providing for strict and effective enforcement of the rules, have reduced the number of shootings.

It is true that police encounters are very often complex and ambiguous making it difficult to make judgments about an officer's culpability. However, there are many occasions of clear and wanton misuse of force. Whenever there is clear evidence of misuse of force and display of brutality by police officers, there should be no hesitation to properly discipline them. If police want citizens to know that police brutality is aberrant, they must isolate officers, who are trigger-happy and prone to violence. This calls for solidarity against and not on behalf of aggressive officers. Protecting the malefactors, through silence and inaction, will not help.

In USA, Black and Reiss, in 1967, made a large-scale observational study on behalf of President's Commission on Law Enforcement and Administration of Justice. In this study, emphasis was placed on detailed descriptions of police vs citizen behaviour, social and demographic characteristics of the participants, etc. In analyzing the data, Reiss found that many instances were there, where the citizens behave antagonistically to police officers and "*many encounters with deviants did not involve uncivil conduct or misuse of force by the police*". However, it has been found that many police officers share the view of the general public that some offenders are despicable people and brutality against them is justified. In India also, downtrodden and marginalized groups become targets of police aggressiveness and their human rights are wantonly violated.

Another factor also influences police overreaction. The expectation of danger in job, has an impact on the attitude and response of a police officer. It has been found that police officers, who face greater dangers in their job, are less inclined to see their job, as helping the citizens in the community. These officers also tend to believe that community is more hostile to them than that actually is the case. This is more so in the case of more prejudiced and less educated officers, who are more prone to overestimate hostility towards them. Similarly, research has also established that police officers, who were less satisfied with their jobs, showed a greater acceptance of physical and verbal abuse of the suspects.

The likelihood of the use of force increases with the bureaucratization of a particular department. It has been found that an officer is more likely to use force, when there are other officers to provide physical and psychological reinforcements.

Training Interventions

Proper and well conducted violence reduction training can have some effect in influencing the conduct and reflexes of the police officers. One of the major purposes of training should be to enable officers to handle their work-related problems better than laypersons. Though training may not compensate for inadequate recruitment of personnel, bad temper and proclivity towards violence are conditions that can be successfully reduced by training. Maintaining one's temper under stressful and confrontational conditions is a skill, that can be taught.

Attitudinal transformation may not be possible by training but the modest goal should be to suppress hostile impulses and replace them by more kindly and positive feelings.

In USA, the case of Monell vs Department of Social Services, established the principle that public employers could be held liable if it could be shown that constitutional violation committed by employees were caused by official customs and practices as well inadequate training.

However, in devising training strategies precautions should be taken not to make matters worse by creating a sense of paranoia among the police officers. During training, officers have to be convinced that there are dangers in police jobs, but such dangers should not be exaggerated. Paranoid officers often overreact with needless violence to minor provocations or no provocations at all. In training programmes, very often some worst case scenarios are presented, but there should also be a strong message that such incidents are usually exceptions in law enforcement.

Further, training for reduction of violence should be continuous. There is need for constant refresher training in violence prevention skills, otherwise, skills learned are likely to atrophy into uselessness. Training should also address the role of police officers during non-working hours. Administrative authorities must define, what they expect off-duty officers to do and to refrain from doing. There are cases of off-duty officers, using their police powers and prerogatives to resolve personal disputes. There are also instances where good faith attempts of officers to intervene in personal disputes or less serious crimes have turned into tragedies.

During training, focus should be on conduct of officer, rather than outcome of the incidents. This is important because interaction between police and the citizens is a two way process. Sometimes, police offices act in inappropriate ways. There might also be outbursts of violence, inspite of reasonable behaviour on the part of the police.

15

Community Policing: Concepts and Elements

Today, community policing has become the buzzword of law enforcement across the world. It has been practiced in many forms and with different results in various countries of the world. John Angell (1971) coined the term "democratic policing" to describe community policing. He called for a change, where citizens have a voice in deciding how police services should be carried out in the community. After all, it is the citizens, who pay taxes that support policing services and they should have a voice in deciding how police services should be carried out in the community.[1] Community policing, indeed, is a reorientation of policing philosophy and strategy, away from the view that police alone can reduce crime, disorder and fear. Police reliance on random preventive patrolling, post-incident investigations to identify and arrest offenders, and other reactive criminal justice system tactics, do not go far in controlling crime and disorder. Community policing implies a basic change in the conception of the role of the police in society. It refers to arrangements of policing that accord a significant role to the community in defining and guiding policing in their locality.

Basic elements of community policing

The key elements of community policing include:

1. Community based crime prevention;
2. Practice servicing as opposed to emergency response;
3. Shifting of command responsibility to lower rank levels and
4. Public participation in the planning and supervision of police operations.[2]

Community based crime prevention involves encouraging and facilitating efforts by the public to take preventive and proactive measures on their own behalf. It grows out of the realization that the first line of defence against crime is not the police, but potential victims. There is the prevailing assumption that citizens can also play an important role in preventing, detecting and reporting criminal behaviour. Reorientation of patrol activities to render non-emergency services is another important element of community policing. It does not mean, as David Bayley says, "police arrogate to themselves social servicing functions carried out by other communities and organizations, but they attend to non-criminal problems and are prepared to assist in constructing solutions, either with an organizational response or a referral service."[3]

Although community policing is first and foremost a crime prevention effort, it does not mean cessation of police efforts to detect crime and arrest and prosecute offenders. Core functions of the police remain unaltered. On the other hand, successful community policing can improve and enhance other police operations by increasing community's cooperation with the police.

Community policing also involves devolution of command responsibility. Community policing, if successfully carried out, should transform the responsibilities of all ranks – subordinate ranks become more self-directing, senior ranks are to encourage disciplined initiatives by junior officers. Skolinck and Bayley refer to the need for a new breed of officer, as well as a new command ethos: "In addition to their traditional duties, community police constables and patrol officers must be able to organize community groups, suggest solutions to neighbourhood problems, enlist the cooperation of people who are fearful or resentful, participate intelligently in command conferences, and speak with poise before public audiences."[4]

Community policing further gives an opportunity to the public to participate in the planning and supervision of police operations. The police officer plays a role of both as an expert and an educator, without forcing the expert opinion on the residents. The citizens provide inputs into defining the problems to be solved, in planning and implementing the problem solving activities and determining if their felt needs have been met. Indeed, at the heart of the community based policing, is the recognition that police are much more than mere crime fighters and can be useful public servants in other ways. The end goal is the creation of a professional, representative, responsive and accountable institution that works in partnership with the public.[5]

In community policing initiatives, building up of partnership between the police and the community is the major challenge. The assumption, that public are keen to develop partnership with police is often not correct. There is invariably community's skepticism that the police are not serious and indulging in some sort of public relations gimmicks. There is also fear of the public that they may have to face reprisals from the criminals, if they closely cooperate with the police. To win public support, the police will have to convincingly demonstrate that they really seek community's help in combating crime and disorder.

Concept of Community

The community, for which the patrol officers are given responsibility, is usually a small, well-defined geographical area or a beat. The community will comprise diverse cultures, values and concerns, particularly, in urban areas. It is also a fact that demands on police for safeguarding one community's interests can sometimes clash with another community's interest. This calls for negotiating skills and suitable organizational efforts on the part of the police. The fact has to be kept in mind that conflicts within the community are as important as their commonalities. Police, in order to function successfully, have to develop a good relationship with all elements of the community and it will centre around the fundamental issues of public safety and quality of life. The effective mobilization of community support requires different approaches in different communities. Establishing trust and obtaining cooperation is often easier in affluent middle class communities, than in poorer communities, where there is longstanding mistrust of the police. Further, alliance within the community should not be limited to some particular incidents or confined to a time frame. It has to be an enduring partnership between the police and the community, in the quest for peace and justice. The police will have to appreciate that people matter and it must empathize with needs, desires and dreams of society.

Problem Solving

Problem solving is another important component of community policing philosophy. It means more than mere prevention of crime. It is based on an assumption that crime and disorder can be reduced in an area by studying the characteristics of problems to deal with them. Community participation in identifying problem and setting priorities will be of help to the community and police. Indeed, many problems in the community, concerning order and security, can be successfully handled by police officers, their supervisors and members of the community. For example, arrangements for better lighting, will reduce instances of petty crimes, like house thefts. Community policing, thus, puts greater emphasis on attacking the underlying causes of crime by addressing them at the grassroot level. These alternative measures will require a wide range of support from the community.

The first step in problem-oriented policing is to move beyond mere handling of the incidents and to recognize that incidents are more often the overt symptoms of substantive problems underlying the complex life patterns of the community. Community partnership will provide police with invaluable insights and inputs. The police will have to understand the nature of problems, as a basis for a critical review of police agencies' response, instead of limiting enquiries to narrower operational goals. Problem-solving, with active support and cooperation of the community, further helps to develop the leadership qualities of patrol officer and enhances his job satisfaction.

Evolution of Community Policing

In later 1970s and early 1980s, police services in England, Japan, Germany, Canada, Singapore were experimenting alternatives to professional bureaucratic model of policing that was widening the gulf between civilians and police officials. In USA, to end police corruption and brutality, there was emphasis upon the professionalisation of police, over a period spanning from 1930s to 1950s. Reforms focused on strengthening of command, control and police arrangement. There was emphasis upon establishing clear chain of command and insulating the police from outside pressures and influence.

A key element of the bureaucratic model was the insulation of the police from political influence. Though the strategy reduced political control of the police, and improved quality and training of the police, it also had the effect of isolating the police from the community. Contact between police and community became limited. It was becoming clear from 1960s, that bureaucratic model was not preventing crime, particularly in the inner cities, and technological advances were distancing police from the community. The police were spending more and more time in fast-moving cars and high-tech equipments. However, Police crime prevention strategies also exacerbated tension between the police and minority communities. There were often accusations from the latter, regarding abusive behaviour, misuse of authority of the police. The only solution bureaucratic model offered to rising crimes was to hire more police personnel and go for more expensive technology. Community policing offered more cost-effective, customer oriented crime preventive approaches.

The professional era also witnessed strengthening of the police subculture. A subculture is comprised symbols, values and beliefs of members of a group in a larger society. The new professionalism of the police created a subculture, setting it apart from the citizens, served and hampered police – community relations. Samuel Walker in his book "Popular Justice" very aptly said that "a half century of professionalisation had created departments that were vast bureaucracies, inward looking, isolated from the public, and defensive in the face of any criticism."[6]

Like most reform movements, community policing in the USA, had its origin in the frustration of an earlier era. Crime, including, violent crimes and drug crimes had risen substantially through the mid 1960s to 1980s, particularly, in American cities. Municipal governments responsible for policing in US, were facing increasing loss of substantial revenues. Private policing was overtaking public policing, to respond to various crimes.

The professional model was also faulted on its failure to provide equitable and impartial policing to all sections of the citizens, particularly, to the minority communities. Black complaints of police misbehaviour and inadequacy of police service, civil rights and anti-war movements also challenged the police. Thus, despite success in 1950s, it became clear that, professional model of policing was not suited to face the changing conditions in 1960s and 1970s, resulting from massive migration of communities in the cities, movements for civil rights, increase of crime and fear and breakdown of informal social control mechanisms all over the country.

Research Studies

Perceptive police officers also carried out a number of field experiments. One such study questioned the value of random patrol propagated by professional model and also revealed that isolation of the police officers in patrol cars created cleavage between the Police and Community. These studies and surveys are milestones in the development of new Police strategies and known as Knwas city Process Patrol Experiments. This partnership was crystallized in the Executive Session on policing, convened by Harvard Kennedy School of Governance from 1984 to 1988. Many of the papers produced from these meetings were jointly written by scholars and police chiefs. Indeed, many of the principles of community policing, appealed more to the academicians than to police officers.

Some potential pitfalls are also associated with community policing. The most serious impediment to community policing programmes, is often police resistance. This spawns from police resistance to innovative change, practices and fear of threat to police autonomy. There is also fear that it may politicize public security functions. Community policing implies not only change of procedures but also a long term reform process that seeks to change the institutional culture of the police.

There is also public apprehension that the police may become too soft on crime and lose the ability to control violence in the community. David Bayley poses the question, "can the police put on a velvet glove and keep their iron hand in shape"?[8] The public may feel that if police become poor crime fighters, they may prove to be ineffective crime preventers. Again, community policing, which seeks to build strong ties between the police and the community, may adversely increase the power of the police in comparison to other government agencies. There is likelihood that, other government agencies may resent the increasing power of the police department. There is also the possibility that community policing may lessen the protection given to unpopular groups, such as, the vagrants and homeless and may even lead to vigilantism. So, before adopting community policing as a mission, police must as Bayley insists, "should know the potential hazards and avoid them". Another paradox noted by scholars and practitioners of community policing is that often well-organized and cohesive community needs community policing the least. Their community policing practices are easiest to implement. One of the common criticisms of the community policing programmes is that they do not make police more responsive to the community rather they increase the police control over the community.

However, the problem is the lack of vision on the part of the police executives, who feel that their authority will be weakened by allowing the field officers, a great deal of discretion. Another challenge, noted by Sadd and Grinc, is that special units, wherever established for community policing, were viewed by some as elitism. "The perception of elitism is ironic, because community policing is meant to bridge the gap between patrol and special units and to empower the rank and file police officer as the most important agent for police work".[9] Indeed, community policing offers a realistic approach to reducing violence and crime and offers a vision for effective policing.

Bayley cautions that "community policing does not represent a small, technical shift in policing; it is a paradigmatic change in the way police operate".[10] Wycoff, while strongly advocating community policing cites Peel's 1829 statement and says that the police are the "only members of the public, that are paid to give full time attention to every citizen in the interest of the community welfare and existence. What we may be seeing is not a new concept under the sun but rather a new sunrise on a fine old concept".[11]

References

1. John E. Angell, "Toward an Alternative to the Classic Police Organisational Arrangement: A Demographic model, *Criminology,* 8 (1971) pp. 185-206 in Quint Thurman, Jihong Zhao and Andrew L. Giacomazzi, *Community Policing in a Community Era: An Introduction and Exploration,* Roxbury Publishing Company, Los Angeles, California, 2001, p.7.
2. D.H. Bayley, (1988), "Community Policing: A Report from the Devil's Advocate, in J.R. Greene and S.D. Mastrofski, Praeger Publishers, New York, p. 226 in Julia Vernon and SandraMcKillop (eds.) *The Police and the Community in the 1990s,* Canberra: Australian Institute of Criminology, p.17.
3. Bayley, D.H. (1986), *NPRU Review,* vol.2, no.2, p.5 in Ibid, p.18
4. Skolnck, J.H. and Bayley, D.H. (1986) *The New Blue Line: Police Innovation in Six American Cities,* The Free Press, New York, p. 4 in Ibid, p. 19.
5. L. Lindholt, P. De Mesquita Neto, D. Titus, and E. Alemika, "Human Rights and the Police in Transitional countries", (Leiden: Brill Academic Pub, 2003, p. 22 in Hesta Groenewald and Gordon Peake, "Police Reform Through Community – Based Policing: Philosophy and Guidelines for Implementation", *International Peace Academy,* September 2004, New York, p. 4.
6. *Samuel Walker, Popular Justice,* (New York: Oxford University Press, 1980), p. 52 in Quint Thurman, Jihong Zhao and Andrew L. Giacomazzi (eds.), *Community Policing in a Community Era: An Introduction and Exploration,* Roxbury Publishing Company, Los Angeles, California, 2001, p. 35.
7. Eck, J.E., and Spelman, W. (1987), *Problem-solving: Problem Oriented Policing in Newport News,* Washington, D.C.: Police Executive Research Forum.
8. David H. Bayley, "Community Policing: A Report from the Devil's Advocate", in *Community Policing: Rhetoric or Reality,* ed. Jack

R. Greene and Stephen D. Mastrofski, 126-237, New York: Praeger Publishers, 1991, p. 228.

9. Susan Sadd and Randolph M. Grinc, *Implementation Challenges in Community Policing: Innovative Neighbourhood-Oriented Policing in Eight Cities,* Washington, D.C., National Institute of Justice Bureau in Brief, February 1996, pp. 1-2.

10. David H. Bayley, "Community Policing: A Report from the Devil's Advocate", in *Community Policing: Rhetroic or Reality,* ed. Jack R. Greene and Stephen D. Matrosfski, 103-20, New York, Prager Publishers, 1991, p. 120.

11. Mary Ann Wycoff, "The Benefits to Community Policing: Evidence and Conjecture", in *Community Policing: Rhetoric or Reality* ed. Jack R. Greene and Stephen D. Mastrofski, 103-20, New York, Prager Publishers, 1991, p. 120.

16

Assessment and Evaluation of Community Policing

Community Policing, in bits and pieces, is now being practised in many counties of the world. Indeed, it has become a buzzword of law enforcement across the world. It represents a paradigm shift in law enforcement and a recognition by the police that community is its best resource and greatest ally in the fight against crime and disorder. However, for the success of community policing projects, there should be in-built mechanisms for periodic evaluations of the program. However, evaluation of community policing policies and practices, poses some difficult problems. The concept has been implemented, in a wide variety of ways, depending on the vision of the police officers, demands and characteristics of the different communities, resource availability and an array of other factors, which contribute to the uniqueness of any community policing programmes. This is because, community policing is not just a uniform set of tasks, it is a philosophy of management and service delivery, which makes an evaluative effort difficult.

A further problem is that, community policing requires administrators, managers, supervisors and officers to think about their responsibilities differently. Reactive and "incident driven" policies have to make way for proactive and innovative ones. Hence, evaluation cannot be done on the basis of merely tabulating the number of calls answered, response time, prosecutions launched, arrests made, etc. This will not give a clear idea of the realization of the goals of the community policing. Further, there is a problem of unanimity. Community policing is implemented in different ways in different areas. There is also significant variability in allocation of resources and deployment of personnel.

Evaluation is necessary for any kind of ongoing projects. It is a necessary step towards a better understanding, if further changes are called for. One of the common points of contention is, whether in the evaluative process, the evaluator is very subjective. It is a fact that very often, an evaluation is not value free, as evaluators become advocates of their own cause. Very often, their results may be justification for the status quo, rather than useful and objective appraisals.[1] There is also the fear of failure and the fear that weaknesses of the programme and implementer may be exposed.

It is also possible that an evaluative study will enable the policy makers, to discover weaknesses in implementation. There may be inherent flaws in the theory or concept itself but there may also be institutional constraints, which are not anticipated or resistance by any of the players, in the implementation process for different reasons. Indeed, evaluation strives to unearth faulty assumptions and continuously redefines goals in the light of information derived during implementation.

The evaluations are carried out either by people working inside the department or evaluators hired from outside. Johnson noted that inside evaluations are not always useful, because some inside evaluators may be tempted or pressured to misrepresent their findings.[2] Outside evaluations are an obvious solution to this problem, because independent evaluators are to use accepted scientific methods to gather data and then report their findings objectively.

Questions for community policing evaluation

Any evaluation of community policing programme should focus on some of these issues:

- What effects will a community policing programme have on residents' quality of life, including, their perceptions of the amount of crime, disorder and fear, they experience?
- What effects will a community policing programme have on actual rates of crime and levels of disorder in a neighbourhood?
- What effect does community policing have on officers, who practice it?
- Is community policing an efficient use of police time and resources?

In USA, some research studies done in the last two decades, have focused on the effectiveness of foot patrol, in reducing crime and fear of crime and improving police citizen relations. Robert Trojanowicz and Dennis Banas found in their case study that foot patrol led to decrease in crime rates, increase in perception of safety and improved police citizen relations over a three-year evaluation period.[3]

Scientific Evaluation

Scientific evaluation means that, it is logical, objective, and has inherent procedures of "quality control", which attempt to ensure the accuracy of the information collected, analyzed, and interpreted in the evaluative process. The type of methodology used, will vary based upon the nature of the program or activities evaluated.

There is always need for rigorous evaluation of community policing strategies, before further expanding them. Evaluation of community policing, will have to focus upon outcome of the programmes. It cannot just rely upon the quantitative analysis of the processes. Apart from noting changes in the crime rate, evaluation should also consider, the level of fear reduction and other least tangible outcomes of improved community police relations. Sometimes, number of cases tends to increase, because of improved relations between the police and community. The increase in reporting is often an indicator of success of improving relationship.

Problems of making evaluation

The common problems found in the evaluation processes are:

1. Very often, police departments which are of bureaucratic and paramilitary nature, rely on uniform procedures.
2. Rigid accountability to the letter of procedures, tends to take precedence over the spirit of procedures,
3. Community policing requires greater flexibility, use of discretion and innovation. Very often, the organization and the people in it find difficult to accept and make the change.

Little feedback, positive or negative, is given to the department's various units on the quality and value of community policing activities. There is, very often, a tendency to keep evaluation results, particularly results, which are intermediately collected in ongoing programs - among the administrative staff. It is not communicated to other supervisors and line level employees, performing the community policing activities. Providing feedback is not only good for program development and implementation it also helps good management.

Further, there should be ongoing communication between different units within the department and different ranks. This will help efficient working of community policing programmes. The communication must be two way - both horizontally and vertically within the organization. Not only leaders should communicate to field officers and line level personnel but there must also be lateral communications between units of the police department. All units of police department must share information, thoughts and ideas as related to their responsibilities and department's goals.

Community policing does require different personnel utilization practices. Programme evaluation must critically examine personnel allocation and deployment decision. There should be long term assignment of personnel with functions along with the commitment of providing supporting resources, to serve in an effective manner.

Departments, while adopting community policing philosophy, must deploy officers to perform activities in support of the philosophy. When policies and practices of the philosophy have been tested, then resources are allotted to operationalize the philosophy. The largest and most well known study in the US, is the evaluation in New York cities (CPOP) programme. The study made significant contribution. It also reflected a common shortcoming in the research in community policing. The evaluators focus mainly on officers and citizens, directly involved in the programme, instead of looking at the effects on the whole community itself.

A series of studies by Brazilian researcher Tulio Kahn, have looked more broadly for impact of community policing on local residents generally and the results were encouraging. Kahn's study of community policing in Sao Paulo suggests that in the neighborhood with community policing, people feel somewhat safer and are more likely to express trust in the police.[4] There is really a need to investigate whether community policing programmes can change people's feelings of security, change their attitudes towards police and enhance willingness to report crimes.

In essence, evaluation of community policing activities is meant to ensure that:

- Activities and processes are effective and accomplish what is intended to be done
- Efficient - they are effective without waste or undue expenditure of resources
- Evaluative processes are valid and reliable
- Timely information is produced within time frames, which makes the information useful for decision-making
- Community policing policies, programmes and activities are all directly related to the department's mission and goals.

Because community policing requires substantially different personnel, utilization practices, any programme evaluation has to examine, effective personnel allocation and deployment decision. Many police departments, when initially adopting community policing philosophy, will deploy more officers to perform activities in support of the philosophy. There is greater flexibility in this kind of experimental deployment.

However, when policies and practices of community policing philosophy have been tested and fine-tuned, resources have to be allocated for operationalising this philosophy. In many ways, allocation can be viewed, as a strategic activity and deployment as more a tactical activity. Indeed, evaluation plays an important role in both allocation and deployment of resources.

Evaluation Reports

Generally speaking, an evaluation report should have three component parts:

(a) Descriptive : The report should describe the issues and processes, which are subject to analysis. The report should also present objectively, all relevant information and data for the users' consumption.

(b) Interpretative: Evaluation should analytically interpret the raw data and information and its impact on issues and activities involved.

(c) Available alternatives : In the light of interpretation, the evaluator must prescribe alternative actions and strategies.

Evaluation reports should also show the ratios of the cost to results and the outcome of programme activities. Overall, programme evaluation is descriptive and not prescriptive. It can also provide alternatives for action. However, it cannot tell what actions to take. Decision making remains basically human responsibility. Evaluation is also programme oriented and not individual-oriented. It examines aggregate issue – cumulative effects of programme, policies and activities and not the individual steps in the process. Further, the programme evaluation is a function in support of organizational goals and not a goal in itself.

US Experience

In USA, elaborate evaluation of community policing programmes and strategies had been done in many areas. The most well known study is the evaluation of New York City CPOP Programmes. In these evaluation programmes, the researchers focused on six police precincts, carrying out community policing programmes. The researchers interviewed the community policing officers at the start of the programme and after six months. The field researchers used a common form (problem – process record) to record how each officer approached the task of problem solving. Based on the information in the form, the field researchers graded the officers on how they handled each problem and the researchers also asked each of the six supervisors to grade their officers. The researchers could then compare the grades given by the field researchers with those given by the supervisors.[5] In New York, the researcher attempted to assess the perception of the community members, by conducting extensive interviews with ten community leaders in each of the six study precincts. The decision to interview community leaders, rather than survey a large number of residents selected at random is partly a matter of cost and also a recognition that most citizens might not have heard of community policing even if its implementation was successful.[6]

Chicago Study

In studies of community policing in Chicago, done by Wesley and others,[7] the researchers surveyed some one thousand five hundred residents, before and after programme implementation and could trace the changes in residents' perceptions about police activity over the periods. The researchers found that some of the groups, who had low opinion about the quality of policing during the pilot period of project, registered slight improvement of the quality of the police service. The researchers also found that the programme did not have any effect on the Hispanic population; they did not participate and also they did not notice any improvement. In Chicago, a large number of officers were also interviewed and it could be seen that black and Hispanic officers were less satisfied with status quo and more optimistic about community policing than white officers. The Chicago researchers, thus, revealed the cleavages within the police department, which mirrored cleavages within the community.

The evaluation of community policing initiatives, have focused on the relationship between strategic problem solving efforts and the fear of crime, crime rates, disorder and satisfaction with the police. Eck and Spelman found evidence that proactive problem-solving approaches, in concert with community members and relevant city agencies, can lead to a reduction in the incidence of specific crimes.[8] Hans Toch and James Grant found that a collaborative approach to problem solving involving the police, residents, and representatives of various city agencies, can curtail neighbourhood social and physical disorder.[9]

Within the evaluation process, the following questions are necessary for the further programme development:

1. *Organization and Development Issues*
- How extensive will resource allocation to various programs be in comparison to the department as a whole?
- Do the crime patterns and service demands in the jurisdiction warrant specializations? If so, what types?
- What is the relationship of community policing activities to other activities in the department?
- Will there be changes needed in the authority and responsibility for community policing activities?
- How comprehensive will community policing activities be?

2. *Administrative Issues*
- What criteria and procedures will be used to target community policing activities and problems?
- What will be the relationship and extent of resource allocation and demonstrable results of community policing efforts?
- On what criteria are community policing goals changed or revised?

3. *Operational Issues*
- How extensive will community policing activities permeate all departmental activities?
- What will the performance measures be and why?

A scientific evaluation may have to be logical, objective and should have inherent procedures of "quality control", which attempts to ensure the accuracy of information collected, analysed, interpreted in the evaluative process. The type of methodology to be used, depends upon the nature of the programme or the activities to be evaluated. Initially, this largely relates to the idea of comparison – the factors against which the comparison made typically fit into the development of the programme so that an effective evaluation can be made.

Types of comparisons may include:

"Real" versus "Expected" Outcomes

It serves as a means to assess the accuracy of projections and forecasts. This can be used to assess the accuracy of hypotheses, conclusions, and recommendations. Actual or "real" results of a program or activity as determined by the evaluation, are compared to the expected results, developed in the planning and development phases of the program/activity.

"Before" versus "After" Status

It examines whether specific activities have had an impact, or contributed to a change in the goals or phenomena peripheral to the goals. For example, measuring burglary rates and citizens' perceptions of safety before a Neighborhood Watch is started and then after the program has been in effect for a year, changes, if any, in the burglary rate and/or the feelings of safety, may be attributed to the Neighborhood Watch.

Contributory Value

The contributory value attempts to assess the degree, to which the programme activities contributed to goal attainment. For example, a community outreach program initiated by the Police department may make citizens more aware of the needs of the public schools or city recreation department. While this may be viewed as a positive effect, it is not related to the police department goals.

Quality Control Assessment

This is an overall, broad-based assessment of the utility, accuracy, general value, orientation, and need of the community policing philosophy and its related programs. As a result, "fine tuning" may need to be made, in order that program and activity quality are reasonably attainable.

Common Problems on Evaluations

Some common problems have been found in the evaluation of police programmes and operations. These are:

1. The department becomes too enmeshed in daily activities and finds difficult to change roles and procedures to

respond to special needs of the department. Being hierarchical and bureaucratic nature, relies heavily on uniform procedures with limited discretion. Consequently, daily activities become routinized. But community policing requires greater flexibility, use of discretion, and innovation. Sometimes, police organizations find difficult to adjust themselves to these changes.

2. Very little feedback, positive or negative, is given to the various units of the department on the quality and value of community policing practices. There is a tendency to keep evaluation results wrapped in secrecy and known only to the administrative staff. Sometimes, even the supervisors of the programme on evaluation do not receive evaluation results.

3. There must be on going communications between all units within the department to make community-policing initiatives work efficiently and effectively. The communications must be two-way-both horizontally and vertically within the organization. All units must share information, thoughts and ideas, as related to their responsibilities and the department's goals. Evaluation methods should be designed to measure the applicable communications related to the programme and activities in question.

Personnel Utility

Community policing requires substantially different personnel utilization practices. Programme evaluation will also be critical to effective personnel allocation and deployment decisions. Resistance to community policing often occurs, when line officers and supervisors believe that the administration does not intend the *real* change. This resistance and cynicism of officers and supervisors will go to reinforce the cynicism of the community.

Researchers also have a role to play in helping law enforcement to develop discreet and realistic goals for community policing - not the laundry list of grand claims that public officials often have to make before launching. In fact, effective programme evaluation is largely dependent upon how well an initiative is thought and developed. It is critical at the outset, to establish a framework, which will be the basis for operations in order to have clear criteria to assess. Meaningful evaluation can be performed only when an initiative has been clearly and comprehensively planned.

References

1. Petersilia, J. 1987, *The Influence of Criminal Justice Research*, Monograph prepared for the National Institute of Justice, US department of Justice, The Rand Corporation, Santa Monica, p. 102.
2. William C. Johnson, *Public Administration: Policy, Politics and practice* (Guliford, CT: Dushkin publishing Group) 1992.
3. Robert Trojanowicz, *An evaluation of the Neighbourhood Foot Patrol Programme in Flint Hills*, Michigan (East Lansing: Michigan State University, National Neighbourhood Foot Patrol Centre), 1982.
4. Tulio Kahn, (2002) "Civilian Oversight of Police", in http://www.altus.org/altus/research_tools/bibliography_ hot_topics.
5. E. McElory, Colleen A. Cosgrove, and Susan Sadd, *Community Policing: The CPOP in New York* (New York, London, New Delhi, Sage, 1993), pp. 12-15.
6. Ibid, pp. 151-53.
7. Wesley G. Skogan and Susan M. Hartnett, *Communiy Polcing:The Chicago Style*, New York and Oxford: Oxford University Press, 1997).
8. John E. Eck and William Spelman, *Problem solving : police oriented policing in Newport News* (Washington DC: Police Executive Research Forum, 1987) p. 250.
9. Hans Toch and James D. Grant, *Police as Problem solvers*, (New York: Plenum, 1991).

17

Community Policing To Foster Community-police Relations

Defining community is not an easy task. Most people recognize community as having positive connotations without giving thought to what exactly it is. Community refers to a specific geographic area, served by the police department or the law enforcement agency and the individuals, organizations or agencies within that area. According to Goldstein, police tend to use the word community, to describe those affected in any way, by the specific problems they are attempting to address or the programmes being launched in response to the problem.[1] According to Klockars, sociologically, the concept of community implies a group of people with a common history, common beliefs and understandings but not always a shared territory.[2] Unfortunately, many communities lack this sense of 'we ness'. As noted by Goldstein, areas of cities, requiring the most police attention are usually those, with few shared values and little sense of community.[3]

The ethnic make up of the community, is one of the most important considerations. A homogenous community is one in which people are, by and large, similar and share similar beliefs and ideas. In heterogeneous community, people are quite different from each other. In modern nation states, most of the communities are heterogeneous, though one ethnic sub-group may wield greater power and control. Establishing and maintaining good relations among the various sub-groups making up the community remains a formidable challenge. Communities are also viewed as a social web, in which people are attached to one another by crisscrossing relationships rather than by one-to-one relationship.

Etzioni on Community

But there is more to the idea of a community, than just interactions with people and a high degree of familiarity among them. In addition to the idea of social bonds, there is also the willingness of the community members to speak up about behaviour they believe is right or wrong. Here Etzioni refers to a community's moral voice, which represents people's commitment to their community, concerning the values they all share. He defines shared values as those beliefs that people hold in common to guide good behaviour and identify bad behaviour.[4]

The moral value is the way that individuals and groups in a good society encourage one another to adhere to norms of conduct that reflect shared values and to avoid behaviour that offends or violates them. The moral voice is often ignored by casual observers because it is informal, subtle, and highly incorporated into daily life. It often works through frowns, gentle snide comments, praise, censure, and approbation. Etzioni suggests that a community demonstrates a strong moral voice, when people speak of their concerns at important moments, that reflect community's values. Once again, it is a matter of social bonds that develop among people, who know one another.[5]

Thus, establishing social bonds and using a moral voice in situations, where shared values being challenged, are key indicators of a strong community. Social bonds also are an important link to law-abiding behaviour. As Travis Hirschi and other criminologists have correctly pointed out that social bonds create attachments to conventional rules and norms, thereby, strengthening social control and consequently keeping people away from violating laws and rules that they might otherwise break. When a system of shared social values or informal social control is weak, society must rely on formal social control and its agents (criminal statutes and law enforcement officers) to regulate criminal behaviour.[6]

Lyon has identified six components that he considers, are the bare necessities for a good community.[7] A good community must provide its citizens with: (i) public safety, (ii) a strong economy, (iii) health care, (iv) educational opportunities, (v) clean, healthy natural environment, and (vi) an optimum population size. In addition to these common objective features, which form the basis for a high quality of life in all communities, Lyon suggests seven more subjective, more debatable components: (a) individual liberty, (b) equality, (c) communal fraternity, (d) representative responsive government, (e) community viability, (f) local identification and (g) resident heterogeneity. Communities differ according to the priorities that they place on each of these seven subjective components.

The weaknesses of police community relations in many parts of the world are today perhaps the greatest obstacle to effective policing. Any improvement in the relationships between the police and the communities will be a vital step towards realizing the goal of better policing. Developments in international policing can provide lessons for the improvement in police community relations. Though different countries have different social dynamics, there are similarities in both the traditions of policing and the forms of social problems encountered worldwide. The area of police community relations (and more recently community policing), has been a major concern to the police forces in different countries of the world. Improved police community relations, will not only lead to greater levels of personal security, but will also have a significant impact on the resolution of community conflicts and the development of more harmonious relationship between various disturbed groups.

Tacit Partnership

According to Van Heerden, there is "*a tacit partnership in policing*, because the very basis of orderliness, is the internalized inclination of every citizen to obey the law. The police are the active partner, with an obligation to convert the passivity of the passive partner, into a full and active partnership".[8] This approach includes some emphasis on the socializing aspect of the police work, which includes the promotion of voluntary compliance to law and voluntary assistance to the police. For example, crime prevention is one of the primary functions of the police. Crime prevention is a broad term, which also includes public education and awareness of steps, to be taken on the prevention of crime. The police can only facilitate the functioning of the components of crime prevention. Its effectiveness depends upon the degree to which the members of the community take responsibility for their own protection and also remain aware of the needs to reduce opportunities for crime.

The community must be willing to cooperate with the police and make available information regarding potential or actual crime problems. Indeed, crime cannot be prevented if the community does not repose confidence in the police to do so. Again at any given time, the number of police personnel is limited. The vast majority of the breaches of law occurs outside the awareness of the police and must be reported to the police, so that they can act on it. It is a fact that success in investigation of cases, contrary to the picture presented in detective novels and crime thrillers, depends not on the professional efficiency of the police investigation but the promptitude of the public to provide information to the police and act as witnesses, when the case comes for trial.

At any given time, both manpower and material resources of the police, are inadequate to cope with the array of problems that confront them and they are pressed hard for many odd jobs, which are not directly their concern. The police have to constantly prioritize their tasks and choice. Resources of the police are everywhere over-extended. Where and how to focus the available resources should be done in a democratic society on the basis of community concerns and community perceptions. Choosing priorities that relate to the real fears of the community, is important in building public confidence in the police. The approach, whereby, the police decide on their own, where their resources should be prioritized, often reinforces perceptions that the police are wasting their time on trivial issues. Where communities are culturally, socially and economically diverse, input into policing priorities is even more important.

Whisenand and Ferguson (1986) have identified three different approaches to interactions, which are initiated in an organized way by the police agencies:[9]

- Public relations are aimed, primarily at informing the public and tend to be one-way communication. Public relations are often concerned with the 'police image'.
- Police community relation is aimed at establishing a dialogue between the police and the community.
- Community policing is a broad term, which involves proactive programmes designed to integrate police community relations with the actual police work.

Different emphasis in these different approaches to police community interaction are reflective of different perceptions of the proper role of the police in the maintenance of social order and of the relationship between police and different communities.

A crisis of policing is often the failure of the relationship, particularly, with the people, who are different, culturally and socially from the dominant group in society. There is also crisis of police developing and growing in a technocratic and paramilitary direction, which serve to isolate the police from the community. Police then rely more on the patrol car and the computer rather than direct vitalizing contact with the people.

It has also been found in many countries that with demographic changes and greater concern for civil rights, particularly, among the minority groups, the police are viewed by the minority groups as tormentors and champions of the status quo. The minority groups feel that the society should offer them same freedom and rights, as those enjoyed by the dominant groups. In Great Britain, the Scarman Report (1989), highlighted the loss of confidence of certain sections of the community, particularly, by many young blacks in the police and underscored the need for police winning their confidence.

For winning the confidence of these disenchanted groups, the police have to seek "the favour and approval of the public at all times and not by pandering to public opinion, but by enforcing the laws with absolute impartiality, giving prompt, individual and friendly service to all members of the society, regardless of status, social position or national affiliation".[10] For successful control of crime in a democratic society, a strong network of community organizations and institutions is called for. This type of cohesiveness will encourage cooperation of the citizens in ways that allow the police to deal with illegal acts better.

In a wider sense, the police community relationship is a form of inter-group relations, as both police and community regard each other as identifiable groups with specific characteristics. Attitudes and perceptions from both police and community tend to be collectively influenced and experiences of the other groups lead to stereotypes being formed.

References

1. Herman Goldstein, *Problem Oriented Policing,* New York: McGraw-Hill Publishing Company, 1990.

2. Carl B. Klockars, "The Rhetoric of Community Policing", in *Community Policing: Rhetoric or Reality*, (eds), Jack R. Greene and Stephen D. Mastrofski, 239-58, New York, Praeger publishing, 1999.
3. Glodstoin, op.cit.
4. Amitai Etzioni, *The New Golden Rule: Community and Morality in a Democratic Society*, (New York, Basic Books, 1996), p.127.
5. Ibid.
6. Tarvis Hirschi, "Causes of Delinquency" (Berkeley: University of California Press, 1969); in Quint C. Thurman, Estimating Social-Psychological Effects in Decisions to Drink and Drive: A Factorial Survey Approach", *Journal of Studies on Alcohol,* 47 (1986) pp. 447-454.
7. Larry Lyon, *The Community in Urban Society* (Philadelphia: Temple University Press, 1987), p. 4.
8. Van Heerden, 1986:53 cited in Etienne Marrais, "Police-Community Relationship", 1992 in http://www.wits.ac.za/csvr/papers/papmar4.htm
9. Paul Whisenand and R. Fred Ferguson, *The Managing of Police Organizations* (Upper Saddle River, NJ: Prentice Hall, 1996), p. 58.
10. Van Heerden, 1986, op.cit.

18

Policing The Police

Policing the police is always a matter of concern in democratic societies. The police are vested with the authority of using legitimate and proportionally justified force against the citizens. This power may be used or abused. The police may use force to protect the rights of the citizens and it may also use it in a manner that imperils the rights and liberties of the citizens. Hence, police powers must be subjected to effective checks and balances. These checks and balances in a democratic system should be perceived as effective and dependable by members of the public.

International experience dealing with police misconduct in different parts of the world shows that exclusive reliance on police self-regulation is not sufficient – capacity of the police to regulate itself is limited and very often does not carry conviction with the people. For this reason, the civilian oversight of the police has emerged as one of the means to exercise checks on police powers. In the United Kingdom, this issue has engaged serious public attention since 1950s. Though the Scotland Yard police traditionally enjoy a good deal of public confidence and respect, there have been in the post-war years, a number of complaints regarding misuse of force and abuse of power by the police. These aberrations brought to the fore the question of police accountability. The Royal Commission of Police in 1962 examined, in depth, the issue of police accountability and on the basis of recommendations of the commission, the Police Act of 1964 was enacted.

Act of 1964

Earlier, when public confidence in police was high, criticisms against the police were muted. But when doubts began to emerge about the proper use of power by the police, it was felt that a more effective mechanism to prevent abuse of power by the police has to be fashioned. The suspicious death of a man in 1962 in police custody followed by other cases of abuse of force by the police like *Sheffield Rhino whip* affair of 1963 colored the debate leading to the Police Act of 1964. Under this Act, the chief constables were required to ensure that all complaints against the police were recorded and properly investigated. In serious cases, investigations will be conducted by investigators from outside the force and all cases in which a criminal offence has been committed will be referred to the Director of Police Prosecution (DPP) for assessment of evidence and prosecution of the offenders.. However, there were accusations of biased and slipshod investigations, as a large number of cases could not be substantiated. It was becoming difficult for the police to convince the critics that their in-house regulatory mechanism was sufficient and police officers were not allowed to escape punishment because of misplaced sympathy.

In 1976, the British government set up a part -time body called Police Complaint Board (PCB) to monitor police investigations. Establishment of PCB evoked strong protests from the police, and particularly, the senior officers. Sir Robert Mark, the well-known Commissioner of London Metropolitan Police, resigned in protest. This watchdog body, however, proved ineffective and somewhat toothless. It failed to command public confidence because of its lack of independent investigative powers and pro-establishment character of its members.

The Police and Criminal Evidence Act (PACE), 1984, swept away the PCB and replaced it by the Police Complaints Authority (PCA). Constitution of the PCA was the outcomo of the enquiry report of Lord Scarman, who enquired into the Brixton riots in April, 1981, when at the center of Brixton hundreds of the young people, not all of them black, attacked the police and indulged in serious acts of vandalism Scarman said in his report that "*law must be sensitively as well as firmly applied. If the police neglect the consultation and co-operation of the local community, unrest is certain and riot becomes probable*".

The PACE (1984) provides that PCA must supervise all complaints related to death or serious injury caused by the police. It is also empowered to do so in other cases of police misuse of power when it considers it necessary in public interest.

The PCA had no separate investigating agencies. It selected police officers from different police force and laid down the requirements for proper conduct for investigations. On completion of investigation, a report is submitted to the chief of the force concerned and the latter is to decide on the basis of the report if the officer has committed a criminal offence or not and whether he should be charged. If a decision is taken to charge the officer, the case is referred to the Crown Prosecution Service (CPS) to decide whether to prosecute the officer.

A major study evaluating the PCA was done by Maguire and Corbett in 1991. The study revealed that the PCA failed to command adequate confidence from the complainants, the police and members of the public. In majority of the cases, allegations of misconduct against the police remained unsubstantiated. The advent of PCA did not bring about any substantial difference in the overall result. In 1989, there were only 765 substantiations out of a total of 9229 cases. Many complainants felt that the PCA was pro-police. Even senior police officers, including, a former police commissioner acknowledged that the PCA had not succeeded in winning confidence of public and the lack of confidence is more prominent among the minority- ethnic communities. This was corroborated in a public opinion survey carried out by the PCA.

Normally, complainants informed after many months that the complaints could not be substantiated, feel discouraged and dissatisfied. Mike Maguire's study shows that some of the complainants were making the first complaints against the police in their lives and felt that it is like *"walking up to a six-feet man". They expect some form of redress or at least an apology or assurance that steps would be taken to prevent a recurrence"*.

Independent Police Complaint Commission

From April 2004, Independent Police Complaint Commission (IPCC) replaced PCA in England and Wales. From May 2000, the British government started consultation on new complaint system for dealing with complaints against police and a consultation document setting out the emerging framework *"Complaints against the police : framework for New System"* was published. This culminated in the Police Reform Act of 2002. Section 9 of the Police Reform Act 2002 established the Independent Police Complaint Commission. Its functions include: (a) handling of complaints made about the conduct of persons serving with police (b) recording of matters from which it appears that there may have been conduct by such persons which constitutes or involves the Commission of criminal offence or behaviour justifying disciplinary proceedings (c) the manner in which such complaints as mentioned in paragraph b are investigated or otherwise handled or dealt with.

Unlike its predecessors, the Independent Police Complaints Commission is completely independent of the police and the Home Office. This change was effected with a view to enhancing public confidence in police service and ensuring greater police accountability. The new system is designed to be more open, just and fair. The Independent Police Commission is a Non-Departmental Public Body (NDPB) funded by the Home Office but by law entirely independent of the police interest groups and the political parties. It has a legal duty to oversee the whole of the police complaint system created by the Police Reforms Act, 2002. Its aim is to transform the way in which complaints against the police are handled.

The IPCC is run by a Chair, a Deputy Chair and 15 Commissioners, each responsible for specific police forces, for guardianship work and for individual cases. Four Commissioners share the responsibility for the Metropolitan Police Service. Commissioners take ultimate responsibility for IPCC investigation, case work and the promotion of public confidence with the complaint system. No member of the Commission may have served as a police officer. Commissioners in making decisions on individual cases act under the delegated authority of the Commission. The Commission meets bi-monthly and dates can be found on the IPCC website. The IPCC is regionally represented in England and Wales through four regional offices.

The Commissioners' code of conduct provides that they should declare any personal or business interests that may influence judgment or appears to influence judgment. The IPCC has teams of investigators headed by Regional Directors in each of its regions to assist with supervision and management of some police investigation. They also carry out independent investigations into serious incidents or allegations of misconduct by persons serving with the police.

The new system means that complaints can be made against anyone working for the police service and not just police officer. This includes police officers of all ranks as well as the support staff, agency staff, who work on behalf of the police. There are also rights of appeal against non-recording of complaints and outcome of police investigations. The complainants will have the right to appeal to the IPCC if; (a) police refuse to record a complaint (b) police stop an investigation against the complainant's wishes and (c) complainant is not happy with how police investigation is carried out. Now copies of investigating officers' reports will be given to the complainant.

IPCC is charged with increasing the efficiency of complaints handling. It seeks to (a) review police investigations to ensure that they remain focused; (b) maximize the value of independent oversight to reach evidence-based conclusions as soon as practicable; (c) be totally independent and consider the needs and position of all throughout the process; (d) in the absence of a public complaint, where appropriate investigate the incident and not necessarily the people concerned and (e) it conducts investigations with due regard for all parties concerned.

Despite being established in April 2004, the first known use of these arrest powers was in 2007, when a former police officer was arrested in relation to allegations of sexual assault. IPCC, since its inception, has so far carried out a number of investigations and supervised more than 1000 enquiries against the police. It has enquired into the shooting of Charles De Menzes, a young electrician from Brazil on 22 July, 2005 by London Police. Earlier, repeated attempts of the police to justify their conduct provoked, a sharp rebuke from the IPCC. The IPCC's decision was that 11 Officers involved in the shooting of the Brazilian will not face disciplinary action. It said that decision whether the four senior officers should be disciplined or not, will be taken after the end of the court procedures. The Crown Prosecution Service previously found no evidence, to warrant the prosecution of any individual over the shooting of Menzes. The family members of Menzes have denounced the decision as "*a travesty of justice and another slap of the face of the family*". The Human Rights Group, Liberty, condemned the delay in deciding whether more senior officers should be punished. However, the Head of the Metropolitan police, Sir Ian Blair thanked the IPCC, after it had absolved all his police officers of any wrongdoing in their killing of Charles Menzes. He described the IPCC report as the "*simple sword of truth*".

In England, the IPCC faces another problem. Police is a beloved institution in England. People are always willing to give police officers the benefit of doubt. The majority of the public in Britain feels that, British police are doing a very fine job under difficult circumstances and they need public support. Criticism of the police is frowned upon by large sections of the public.

19

Encounter Speciality Debases Ethicality

The murder of the Assistant Commissioner of Delhi Police, Rajbir Singh, raises a few disturbing issues concerning policing and law enforcement. Rajbir Singh, who had eliminated some dreaded gangsters and militants in high profile encounters, was a flamboyant officer of Delhi police. He was a brave and tough officer, whose work was lauded by his superiors, enabling him to get quick promotions. As reported in the press, he was winner of President's Gallantry Medal and other decorations. However, as happens in the case of many ambitious police officers, he did not care for rules and norms and got enmeshed in many controversies. There were allegations that he was involved in shady deals with builders and promoters. It is not clear whether he was killed by a builder during a tiff or there was a well-laid conspiracy to murder him. Further, police investigation will unravel the truth.

Rajbir earned name and notoriety as a sharp-shooting-encounter-specialist. He won appreciation from the departmental bosses as well as from the public for his dare-devilry. In our country, the public also love tough, extralegal action against the criminals, who are escaping conviction and getting away scot-free because of the malfunctioning of the criminal justice system. Public, and particularly, the educated middle class, do not mind if in the process, police start taking laws into their own hands and become executioners themselves. There is also pressure on police officers in the field from political masters, and even departmental superiors, to show quick results by means fair or foul.

The slow moving criminal justice system of the country compounds the police dilemma. Trials drag on indefinitely in courts of law. Witnesses are easily gained over and turn hostile. Criminals are able to escape punishment by devious means and feel further emboldened to carry on their nefarious operations. The police, thus, face tremendous pressure to adopt extra-legal and shortcut means from the political bosses and departmental superiors and also from the members of the public. Indeed, encounters are not the problem but symptoms of a collapsing criminal justice system. Civil libertians presume that all extra-judicial killings stem from the bloodthirstiness of the police themselves; but this is not always the case. Police are encouraged to do the dirty work of the society because the criminal justice system is not functioning and overhauling the entire system of justice is too big a task.

In many state police forces, there are now encounter specialists, who become darlings of political masters and police bosses. In the name of firmly dealing with the dreaded criminals and terrorists, they turn into cold-blooded liquidationists. The heady wine of power and success turn their heads and many of them become corrupt. They turn into extortionists, who enrich themselves by dubious means. It is alleged that ACP Rajbir Singh, who had developed a nexus with the promoters and builders, was ultimately hoist with his own petard. The violent and corrupt propensities of these officers were not unknown to the senior officers of the organization, but they are lionized because by adopting the extra-legal methods, they deliver the goods. Unfortunately, when troubles thicken, they are cast away by their political and organizational bosses. Recently in Gujrat, the well known encounter specialist D.G. Vanzara found to his utter dismay that the Chief Minister and political leaders, who were appreciating his work earlier, dumped him because they wanted to present an untarnished image before the Supreme Court. Like cardinal Wolsey, Vanzara had to rue his unthinking loyalty to the king. Similarly, Rajbir's departmental and political patrons have quietly distanced themselves from this unseemly case. It is reported in the press that in his funeral ceremony, there were no wreaths from his senior officers. Only a junior officer represented Delhi police.

In every police force, there are some violence-prone officers who repeatedly figure in abuse and misuse of force. In USA, Christopher Commission, which looked into the misuse of force by the police after the Rodney King incident in Los Angles, could pinpoint a few officers, who are frequently involved in blatant misuse of force. There should be no hesitation on the part of police leaders to discipline, and if necessary, to weed out these black sheep.

Unfortunately, there is supervisory cowardice. Senior officers often fail to muster courage to pull up their aberrant subordinates who often enjoy political patronage. Further, supervisory cowardice is compounded by systemic arrogance, which generates a belief among many officers that they have the right to use power and influence to punish anyone posing, according to their perceptions, threats to public order and safety.

In Indian police, peer group supervision is also conspicuously missing. Peer supervision can be a powerful tool for ensuring police accountability and all-round good policing. In Japan, police officers work in pairs with the understanding that one officer is responsible for ensuring the correct work and conduct of the other. In India also, policemen work in groups but the ethos is against the assumption of mutual responsibility. Peer supervision is closer and better informed than supervision by senior officers. But it has unfortunately remained a neglected aspect of internal regulation.

In this connection, it is to be borne in mind that encounter per se is neither illegal nor undesirable. The police and security personnel, when attacked by criminals and terrorists, can exercise the right to private defense. Genuine encounters for the purpose of dealing with dangerous criminals and terrorists, come within the framework of law with reference to sections 97, 100 and 103 of IPC, which deal with the private defense of life and property. Thus, legal provisions do exist to justify use of force against criminals and terrorists, which may even result in causing of their death. But fake encounters have to be sternly discouraged. The National Police Commission (Fifth Report) strongly recommended that false encounters are to be discouraged because this is not the remedy for the situation. The answer is to strengthen law and legal processes. Violating the rule of law in the name of law enforcement is not desirable even from the limited police point of view. There are instances where criminals have used the police to bump off their rivals in intra gang warfare. Research has shown that notorious Dawood Ibrahim got many of his rivals eliminated through the police by tipping them in advance. Police arrived on the scene not for arresting but eliminating the criminals.

In police profession, there are many, who mistakenly think that end justifies the means. However, the point to be kept in mind is that adoption of impermissible means ultimately undermines the end. The practice of policing to break law in the name of law enforcement will be arbitrary as a process and random in its effect. Further, violating the rule of law will have the effect of "*scapegoating*" the police. Police officers, and particularly, the police leaders have to remember that when police takes recourse to extra-legal tactics to make up the deficiencies of law and legal procedures, they are trying to remedy the inadequacies that they did not create. Further, illegality in the service of public safety as Dr. David Bayley puts it, "*makes policing a furtive and anxious activity and undermines pride which is the basis of job satisfaction*". And the most effective means of changing the mindset of police officers will be to convince the police leaders that violating the rule of law is not a sound law enforcement. They should be encouraged to change the moral tone and management priorities within the organization to convince the rank and file that extra-legal methods are counter-productive.

20

Vigilante Justice

Incidents of mob justice are becoming quite common. Lynching of so-called criminals and miscreants has increased all over the country. It has become a new crime wave. Recently, at Nawada in Bihar, (September 9, 2007), an angry mob gouged out eyes of three teenagers, who had snatched a motorbike from a local resident. In Bhagalpur, a young man was almost beaten to death by a mob, after being accused of chain snatching. He was then chained to a motorcycle by policemen and dragged along in full view of television cameras. Even children are not being spared. In a shocking instance in Nawada, two children were beaten up and paraded in the streets with their heads tonsured because they stole packets of detergents from a shop, where they were employed. A number of incidents of lynching of criminals have been reported from Jharkhand.

The growing number of incidents of quick and rough mob justice show that the people no longer repose faith in the criminal justice system of the country, which has become slow moving, cumbersome and effete and have started in believing in

"Vigilantism" – taking law in their own hands and delivering instant justice. This is an ominous trend and augurs ill for law enforcement and order maintenance in the country.

The word vigilante is of Spanish origin and means *"watchman"* or *"guard"*. When someone is taking law in his own hands, he is supposedly engaged in vigilantism. The first American vigilantes called themselves *"regulators"*, because they viewed their action as restoring balance to a situation, that was out of control.

Police are often blamed for the rising trend of vigilantism. It is true that police alertness can prevent some cases of lynching of criminals but the reason for this growing phenomenon lies elsewhere. Today, the country is witnessing a surge in crime and lawlessness. In states like Bihar, vast rural areas remain under-policed and at the mercy of lawless elements. In India, in the year 2004, as many as 6028781 cognizable crimes had been reported. When compared to 2003, the crime rate increased by 7.9%. But the fact of the matter is that there is massive burking of crime. Even by a very conservative estimate, actual incidence of crime should be ten times more then what it is reported. Non-registration of cases by the police, particularly, in the rural areas, is very common. It is a grotesque violation of human rights and forces many people to take laws in their own hands and punish the criminals.

One very important reason for non-registration as forcefully highlighted by the National Police Commission in its report, is the anxiety of the political executive of the state government to keep the crime figures low, so as to claim before the state legislature, the public and the press, that the crime is well under control as a result of efficient police administration under their charge.

However, even the suppressed crime figures cannot conceal the hard fact that violent crimes are increasing. The difficult and deteriorating crime situation is further compounded by the fact that most of the criminals go unpunished. Figures of disposal of cases in the courts of law, compiled by the National Crimes Record Bureau for the year 2004, show that 83% of IPC cases remain pending trial in various criminal courts of the country. It is evident that trials conducted by the courts have not kept pace with time. Though the over-all conviction rates in respect of criminal cases is 42%, but conviction in respect of heinous crimes as pointed out in the report of Malimath Committee, is just 10%. The sieving process of the criminal justice system is operating more in favour of the offenders. There is imperative need for quick, affordable and incorruptible justice to the people. Otherwise as K R Narayanan, former President of India observed, "*the people instead of turning to courts of law will take law in their own hands.*"

It is a fact that vigilantism, however, controversial, always enjoys a considerable degree of ground level support. But organized group vigilantism can become dangerous. It occurs, when there is a perceived weakness in the ability of the formal criminal justice system to respond promptly to deal with the crime and violence. So long as this gap remains, vigilantes seek to take on responsibilities of the formal criminal justice system. In the event of prolonged and widespread vigilantism (as is the case in Bihar), vigilantes seek to usurp power reserved for the Criminal Justice System.

Sometimes vigilantism is wrongly equated with self-defense. Vigilante behaviour is premeditative while self-defense is spontaneous. Vigilante mindset is often the very opposite of "*due process mindset*", as the vigilantes do not care for the police to finish their investigation and courts to punish the offenders. What they care about is quick, final and cost effective justice. They do not seek vengeance. They are not avengers. They seek swift and sure punishment. Lynch mob, as psychologists point out, armour themselves with a sense of retributive righteousness. They mean to exert social control by exemplary doses of terror on the notion that the violence is the only language that the victims understand. Each atrocity has its own circumstances, its own atmosphere and triggers.

It has been found that established vigilante groups can be of two kinds - crime control vigilantes and social control vigilantes. The crime control vigilante group seeks to punish those, who they believe are guilty of criminal wrongs (i.e., thief, outlaws, and fugitives from justice). The social control vigilante group seeks to repair some transgression in the social order that threatens to affect the communal values and sense of honour. In Islamic societies, the practice of honour killing, when a female member of the household shames the family name, is a widely tolerated vigilante activity.

Vigilantism also arises from a policing vacuum. The vigilantes perceive that the police are either unable or unwilling to control certain criminal behaviour. It will be possible for the police to outline carefully and explicitly what they currently do or attempt to do to control criminal behaviour and what strategies they want to adopt for dealing with it.

While the vigilantes feel antagonistic towards the police, quite often the reverse is not the case. A fact, which is sometimes overlooked is that vigilantism can be quite popular among the police officers. Research studies of vigilante groups in New York by Kenney, found that many police officers approved the vigilante groups and their methods. There are known instances where police officers join with the mob and encourage them to take law in their own hands and mete out instant justice to the criminals. I know of a case, where an officer in charge of a police station got rid of two notorious criminals of his jurisdiction by inciting a mob to lynch them. This kind of perversity is now increasingly being displayed by many other police officers.

It is also a fact that the temptation to take law into one's own hands is much greater when people believe that they can get away playing vigilantes. It is necessary for the police and political authorities to deal firmly with the vigilantism, making clear that this form of criminal activity will be put down firmly. "Do it yourself justice" represents a serious threat to the democracy and to the rule of law, which cannot be countenanced.

21

Jessica Lal's Murder: A Case of Criminal Injustice

Acquittal of all the accused persons in the sensational 7-year old Jessica Lal murder case has rudely shocked the conscience of the civil society and shattered its faith in the working of the criminal justice system. A Delhi court acquitted all the accused persons stating that the police have failed to prove its case. News items and articles have appeared in the press, highlighting glaring lapses and loopholes in the investigation of the case like non-recovery of the weapon of offence, non-seizure of the wearing apparel of the murdered victim, conflicting ballistic theories and deliberate tampering of evidence. There are apprehensions and insinuations that the investigators deliberately, at the instance of the rich and powerful (main accused Manu Sharma, is the son of a Haryana Minister), botched up the case.

However, the job of the trial court does not end as the Supreme Court has observed (case of Mir Mohammed Omar and others), by picking up lapses in investigations and expressing unsavoury criticisms against the investigating officers. The apex court said that, the trial court should bear in mind the time "*constraints of the officers in the present system, ill equipped machinery that they have to cope with and the traditional apathy of respectable persons to come forward and give evidence in the criminal cases. These are the realities, the police forces have to confront while conducing investigation in almost all cases.*"

This open-and-shut case failed in the court of law for a variety of reasons. Besides shoddy investigation, another very important reason is that the eye witnesses present at the Tamarind Court Restaurant, who witnessed the gruesome murder of Jessica Lal, were pressurized, gained over and turned hostile. Actor and model Shyam Munshi, an eyewitness to the murder of Jessica Lal, told the police that he saw Manu Sharma firing at Jessica Lal but made an U turn and stated before the court that Sharma was not the shooter. There were two other persons who shot at Jessica. Similarly, Shiv Das, an electrician at Tamarind Court told the police that he saw Manu Sharma having an argument with Jessica and then firing at her. But he turned hostile and said before the court that he entered the hall only after he heard the shot and did not see the assailant. There were many other respected and responsible figures present but none came forward to depose truthfully before the court.

Witnesses turning hostile, though deplorable, are not uncommon. Indeed, there are various reasons for witnesses turning hostile and not deposing correctly in a straightforward manner. The first, the manner of conducting investigation by the police is often rude, overbearing and inconsiderate. Many witnesses feel discomfited. Second, cases drag on in the courts interminably with frequent adjournments and very little regard is paid to the convenience of the witnesses. A belief prevails even among many educated people that to get embroiled as a witness is like being played as a fish on a long line. This case dragged on for more than 7 years and delay ordinarily prejudices the prosecution. Witnesses become non-available and the accused persons, particularly, the rich and the powerful (as happened in this case), utilize all available means to gain over the witnesses. The innocent person, who dares to speak, may incur the wrath of the hardened criminals and lose their lives and limbs. Third, there prevails a belief in public mind in the Indian society that the individual has no responsibility in assisting the police in criminal matters. Prevention and investigation of the crime is the sole responsibility of the police. This kind of myopia also prevails in other countries but it is more acute and pronounced in India.

This brings to the fore the need for effective witness protection programme. As early as in 1962, Maharashtra Police Commission made a special point of the need to give protection to the witnesses, who testify against the gangsters. The Malimath Committee Report on Reforms of Criminal Justice System (2003) also emphasised the urgency of effective witness protection programme. There is utmost need for providing protection to the witnesses in very important cases, where they apprehend dangers to their lives. In this connection, it may be mentioned that in the USA Federal Witness Protection Programme was created in response to threats faced by the witnesses, who testified against the mobsters and the programmes have been in existence in America since 1967. Round-the-clock protection is provided to all witnesses through the US Marshal Service, who fear threats for their lives. It has so far been used to rehabilitate 8000 witnesses and their 15000 family members. Recently, Canada gave witness protection cover under its Witness Protection Act, 1996, to a Sikh woman, who threw fresh light on Kanishka Bombing Case.

162 CrPC

The provisions of criminal law, based on the distrust of the police encourage this foul game by the witnesses and affect the fate of the cases. Section 162 of the CrPC provides that the statement recorded by the police in the course of investigation, shall not be signed by the person making the statement. This kind of ban on witnesses signing their own statements stems from the same distrust of the police that makes confession before the police inadmissible in evidence, (Section 25 of Indian Evidence Act). This enables the witnesses to frequently resile from their statements made before the police in a court of law. In England, statements made before the police are generally signed by the witnesses and considerable importance is attached because it is difficult to confute such statements. The Law Commission in its 14th Report (Vol. II) recommended that a statement by the witness is to be reduced in writing and signed by him, provided the witness is capable of reading what has been recorded. The Commission observed *"Psychologically, persons, who witness the commission of an offence are eager to state the true version, if they are questioned soon after the commission of the offence before consideration of influence has worked on them"*. The Punjab Police Commission also opined that Section 162 of the CrPC should be amended as recommended by the Law Commission. The Malimath Committee observed that frequent change in statements by a witness during the course of investigation and trial, results in miscarriage of justice. There should be tape recording or video recording of statements of witnesses dying declaration and confessions. These facilities did not exist at the time when the basic laws of the land were enacted Now these facilities being available to the investigating agencies, should be optimally utilized.

Again, if a witness turns hostile during trial proceedings, it is the duty of both the prosecutor and the judge, to cross examine the witness and ascertain whether he or she turned hostile because of fear or any other ulterior considerations. If this proves to be so, the statement can be ignored and a retrial ordered. This was precisely done by the Supreme Court in the Best Bakery case.

Tendency for a judge presiding over a trial to assume the role of a referee or an umpire in a cricket match, allowing the trial to develop into a contest between the prosecutor and the defence, have been deprecated by the Supreme Court. This can be achieved, as the Malimath Committee has correctly observed, by mandating the court to become active seekers of truth. Quest for truth should be the hallmark of the criminal justice system. A Judge has to be proactive. Section 311 of CrPC of 1973 provides that the courts at any stage of enquiry, trial and other proceedings, may summon any person as a witness, examine any person present, though not summon as witness or recall any person already examined, if his evidence is necessary for a just decision. But Section 311 of 1973 code remains a dead letter. Rarely the magistrate or a sessions court judge summons on his own, witnesses in a criminal case. He behaves like an impartial referee and this is what the judge precisely did in Jessica Lal's case. The Malimath Committee's recommendation to amend section 311 CrPC, to make it obligatory for the courts to recall or reexamine, at its own initiative, any person already examined has not just been translated into law.

Perjury

Witnesses also make false statements in courts without any fear. Unfortunately, there are no hard data on the extent and incidence of perjury. Prosecution and convictions for perjury are few and far between. There is a telling folk tale in Karnataka "*speak the truth since you are not telling in a court of law*". The Malimath Committee felt that, while in New York state, the punishment for perjury has been enhanced to 15 years, in our country, the offence of perjury has been dealt with very leniently. The Malimath Committee recommended that section 344 of the CrPC, may be amended to require the court, to try the perjury cases summarily, once it forms an opinion that the witness has knowingly and willfully given false and fabricated evidence. It is unfortunate that the Criminal Law Amendment, passed by the Parliament to prevent the evil of witnesses turning hostile, did not contain the recommendations of the Malimath

Committee for summary processes of trial of witnesses deposing contrary to statements recorded under section 164 A by a Magistrate.

Another important recommendation of the Malimath Committee was that the victims should have the right to appeal and be represented by a lawyer. If the victim is an indigent person and not in a position to engage a lawyer, the state should provide him a lawyer. When the state has an obligation to provide a lawyer to the accused, there is no reason that the victims should not be provided with a lawyer at the cost of the state. This also does not find place in the Criminal Law Amendment Act.

It is also equally important to insulate the investigation as well as the prosecution wings from extraneous pressure and influence. Charges have been levelled against the police for partisan investigation in Jessica Lal case and so many other cases at the behest of the rich and influential politicians. Hence, institutional mechanisms in the form of National and State security commissions, as recommended by the National Police Commission as well as the National Human Rights Commission, have to be devised. This crucial recommendation should be incorporated in the new Police Act for the preparation of which, a committee has been set up under Soli Sorabjee. Indeed, in our country, though judiciary is independent, the judicial processes are not. The independence and fairness of the judiciary will have no meaning to the citizens in the criminal matters, if the police, who prepare the matters for adjudication in the courts, are subjected constantly to corrupting influences. A clean and non-politicized police is as important as an independent judiciary for the ultimate health of the criminal justice system.

Now the Delhi High Court has stepped into the breach and called for a detailed report from the Delhi Police on what went wrong in the case. It is hoped that this will lead to retrial of the case. The shameful episode of Jessica Lal's case should spur demand for meaningful and pragmatic reforms of the criminal justice system.

22

Nothing But The Truth

There is a pressing need to enforce perjury laws in India as stringently as possible. In a growing number of cases, witnesses are turning hostile and stating exactly opposite of what they had earlier stated before the police, and sometimes even before the Magistrate. In the latest twist, in BMW hit and run case, a sting operation has exposed as to how an important witness was sought to be gained over by the defence lawyer as well as the prosecutor.

Perjury is a criminal offence of making false statement's under oath. It is a crime that occurs when an individual wilfully makes a false statement during a judicial proceeding after he/she has taken an oath to speak the truth.

Perjury in India has become common because there is very little danger of getting punished. The sanctity of oath in the courts has disappeared and witnesses make false statements in the courts without any compunction. There are no hard data on the incidence and extent of perjury. Prosecutions are few and far between and hence the available data hardly reveal a clear picture.

Malimath Committee (2003) in its report on Reforms of the Criminal Justice System dealt with various aspects of the problem elaborately. The report enumerated the difficulties and inconvenience encountered by the witnesses in the courts of law. In most of the courts, there is no designated place, with proper arrangements for the witnesses for seating and resting, while waiting for their turn to be examined as a witness in the court. It is a fact that witnesses are treated with scant respect and consideration in the courts of law. Cases drag on interminably with frequent adjournments and very little regard is paid to the convenience of the witnesses. This kind of myopia also prevails in other countries but it is more pronounced in India, because its citizens are submerged in their small family and community circles and their foremost duties are confined within these circles.

Witnesses give evidence in criminal courts after they are administered oath or affirmation as per the Oaths Act 1969. Section 8 of the Oaths Act provides that the witnesses are bound to state the truth on the subject. The sanction behind the oath is supposed to be the fear of God or fear of eventual punishment by God. But in practice, the witnesses make statements without slightest regard for the oath or affirmation that has been administered to them. It seems that the administration of oath or affirmation gives virtually licence to the witness to make false statement to before the court with impunity.

Perjury can seriously subvert the course of justice and cause conviction of a wrong person, while a perjurer can get away with impunity. Perjury is a penal offence under sections 193 to 195 in the Indian Penal Code for which adequate punishment has been prescribed. Section 195 (b) of Criminal Procedure Code (Cr.P.C.) prescribes that no court shall take cognisance of perjury under section 193 to 195 IPC except on the complaint in writing of the court. Section 340 CrPC provides for procedure to be followed for making a complaint contemplated by section 195 Cr.P.C. The procedure is somewhat convoluted and long-drawn. Section 344 Cr.P.C. however, provides an alternative summary procedure empowering the Court of Sessions or Magistrate First class to try the witness summarily and sentence the perjurer to imprisonment, which may extend up to three months or a fine of Rs. 500 or with both. The provision is seldom resorted to by the courts. Indeed, the response of the courts in dealing with the serious problem of perjury has been so far tepid and borders on indifference.

Offering false testimony in a criminal trial is a serious offence that undermines the integrity of the criminal justice system. Instead of truth, falsehood prevails. The punishment prescribed for perjury is also lenient. In USA, under the federal laws, a sentence of 5 year's imprisonment is provided for perjury. Now in the state of New York, the sentence for perjury has been raised to 15 years. In western countries, many well-known persons have been convicted for perjury – something unheard-of in India. They include Jeffrey Archer, British novelist and politician sentenced to 4 years of imprisonment and Jonathan Atkins, British politician, who was a member of John Major's cabinet, sentenced to 18 months' of imprisonment for perjury. Very recently, Lewis Scooter Libby, former aide to Vice President Dick Cheney, was convicted on 2 counts of perjury along with other offences in connection with Palme Affairs. The Criminal Law Amendment Bill introduced in Parliament in 2003, was designed to prevent the evil of witnesses turning hostile by inserting new sections to ensure that the evidence of central witnesses was to be recorded by the Magistrate in certain cases, where investigation is of an offence punishable with death or imprisonment for 7 years, and also under consideration was summary procedures for the trial of witness deposing contrary to statements recorded by the magistrate. Unfortunately, the provision was not passed by the Parliament. They were omitted from the final Act since the Select Committee decided to "drop" these provisions. Fali Nariman calls it "*a most unfortunate decision*".

Widespread prevalence of perjury is symptomatic of the inadequacies and ailments bedevilling the Criminal Justice

System of the country. One glaring inadequacy is the lack of any witness protection programme, which very often inhibits the witnesses from coming forward to depose against the rich and the powerful. They are threatened and pressurized and often out of fear of life and limbs resile from their previous statements. Malimath committee in its report (2003) urged the government to enact a law for giving protection to the witnesses and their family members on the lines of similar law prevalent in US and other countries. In USA, Federal witness programme was created in response to threats faced by the witnesses to testify against the mobsters and the program has been in existence since 1967. Round-the-clock protection has been provided to all witnesses, who fear threats to their lives through the US Marshal Service. It has been used so far to rehabilitate some 8000 witnesses and their 15000 family members. Canada gave witness protection cover under its Witness Protection Act, 1996 to a Sikh woman who threw fresh light on Kaniska Bombing Case. Witness protection programme is the need of the hour and we have to start with the programmes, however small, immediately to prevent witnesses from turning hostile. The Witness Protection Guidelines issued by the High Court of Delhi in the case of Neelam Katara vs. GOI and others (2003) could be a starting point in this direction.

23

Forgotten Victims

In our criminal justice system based upon Anglo-Saxon adversarial pattern, the victims of crime are very often forgotten and neglected. During the last 100 years, there have been far reaching changes in criminal justice systems concerning the rights of the accused during the investigation of crime, prosecution of the offenders and punishment to the accused in the event of misconduct. Statistics on the offenders, details of arrest by the police administration and release of criminals from the penal institutions are all kept. But very often, collection of various aspects of information relating to the victims remains neglected. When a citizen commits a crime, he questions the authority of the state. In the process, the focus of the state shifts from the victim, who has suffered loss and injury, towards the offender. The victims are marginalized and the state stands for the victims to punish and prosecute the offenders.

After the II world war, in countries like France, Germany, U.K. and USA, there emerged a progressive school of thought in criminal justice system, which tried to shift the focus of attention to victims, who deserve redress and very often, fail to get it. The historical evolution of the penal system from private vengeance to the state administration of justice, resulted in a criminal justice system, in which the victims play a very secondary role.

According the U.N. General Assembly Resolution (General Assembly Resolution, 40/34, November 29, 1985), victim means person or group of persons, who individually or collectively have suffered harm, including, physical or mental injury, emotional suffering, substantial impairment of the fundamental rights, through acts or omissions that are violation of criminal laws operating in member states. The UN Declaration for Basic Principles for Victims of Crime and Abuse of Power, was adopted by the General Assembly at its 19th Plenary Meeting on November 29, 1985. The Declaration emphasized the need for assistance to the victims of crime at all stages and specified basic standards of treatment for them.

Insensitivity Of The Police

In the prevailing criminal justice system in India, the victim faces various problems and handicaps. He is summoned to the court repeatedly. Inherent delay and frequent adjournments, expenditure in the court processes and uncertainty of getting justice in spite of all the ordeals, are some of the issues, which confuse the minds of the victims. The most common and frequent problem faced by many of the victims, while reporting a case is, absence of receptive and sympathetic attitude of the police towards the victims. The traumatized victim comes to the police station with great mental stress. He is often treated with total lack of courtesy and sensitivity. Victims experience great difficulties in getting cases registered. Even after registration, investigation is done very carelessly and in slipshod manner because of the multifarious commitments of the police officers or due to ulterior motives. The presumption that the prosecutor adequately represents the victim is often not correct. It is contradicted by the reports of many victims. Very often, whether the offender will be prosecuted or not, is influenced by considerations other than the interests of the victim. It is also known that prosecutors often do not disclose the impact of crime on the victim and his family to the sentencing authority.

In America, the growing perception is that the criminal law should be responsive to the needs of the victims was eloquently expressed by the President's Task Force on Crime (1982), which asserted that "*Victims, no less than the defendants are entitled to their day in courts. Victims no less than the defendants are entitled to have their views considered. A judge cannot evaluate the seriousness of a defendant's conduct without knowing how the crime has burdened the victim*".

Court Procedures

Victims often find the court procedures as cumbersome and frustrating. The criminal trial takes the form of offender versus the state. If the victim often feels that nobody cares for his suffering, it is actually so, because institutionally nobody does. The victim and the defendant have to stand as witnesses during the trial, but the victim unlike the defendant, can be subjected to severe cross-examination by both the counsels. Research work on the subject done in various countries have shown that the victims demand not only compensation or the punishment of the offenders, they also wish to be recognized as important and necessary participants in the criminal justice system. To be heard is as important as being compensated.

Some kind of victims' integration in the criminal justice process have been tried in many countries. In USA and parts of Canada, the right has been granted, in the use of Victim Impact Statement (VIS), which is a statement made by the victim and addressed to the judge. It contains the description of the harmful financial, social, psychological and physical consequences of the crime on the victim. It also includes the statement, concerning the victim's feelings about the crime, the offenders and the proposed sentences. It has been argued in favour of the VIS that the effectiveness of sentence will increase, if the court knows the feelings and agonies of the victim. But others have contended that victims may turn out to be vindictive and the objective approach of the court may be influenced by the subjective pressure of the victim. The research work done by the US Justice department, however, shows that less than 10 per cent of the victims reported crime in order to see that the offender is punished. Very often, the victims want compensation, help and consultation rather than heavy punishment. In United States, the Supreme Court ruled that consideration of VIS during sentence hearing was constitutionally permissible (Payne versus Tennesse, III S.Ct. 2597 (1991).

Research studies on victims participation in criminal justice process has also revealed that it has both negative and positive advantages. The advantages are, as some have argued, that the sentencing will be more accurate, if victims convey their feelings and the criminal justice process will be more democratic and better reflect the community's response to crime. But opponents have alleged that a gain for the victim is a loss for the defendants. Because victims are believed to be vindictive and unforgiving, it is assumed that their participation will result in harsher sentences[1]. Some jurists have also opined that to bring victims back into the criminal process is to revert to the eye for an eye system that inappropriately breaks down the distinction between civil and criminal law.

In USA, the President's Task Force on Violent Crime in 1981, recommended the development of federal legislation that would establish federal Office for Victims of Crime in the US Department of Justice and federal funding, to support state victim compensation programmes and local victim assistance programme. The Victims of Crimes Act-1984 established crime victims fund, based on the collection of fines from the federal criminals. It also recommended establishment of the Attorney

General's Task Force on Family Violence in 1983. Its 1984 report stimulated, federal action requiring state compensation programs to cover victims of family violence, who receive federal funds. It further recommended, an amendment to the US constitution according victims the right to be present and heard at all critical stages of judicial proceedings.

Compensation To The Victims Of Crime

International Covenant on Civil and Political Rights (1976), indicates that an enforceable right to compensation, is conceptually integral to human rights. Article 9(5) of the Covenant lays down "*any one who has been the victim of unlawful arrest or detention shall have an enforceable right to compensation*". Switzerland had a scheme of compensation to victims of crime since 1937. Subsequently, other states like UK, USA, have passed victims of crime compensation schemes. In England, the penal reformer *Margery Fry* in 1960s, propounded the concept that the state should provide financial reimbursement to the victims of violent crimes. New Zealand, was the first state to adopt a victim compensation programme in 1963. Similar laws were passed in Great Britain and different states in USA. The victim-oriented criminal justice gained international recognition with the adoption by United Nations, of the Declaration of Basic Principles of Justice for Victims of Crime and Abuse of Power. This UN document encouraged other nations to pass laws, expanding the rights of the victims. It has been suggested by some scholars that compensation schemes may be financed from fines or prison wages. This has already been done in Italy, where under a 1974 Act, three-tenths of the prisoner's earnings go to the victims of crime[2]. However, these funds are not adequate. Besides, deduction from a prisoner's wages are liable to be detrimental to his rehabilitation and involve hardship for his family. A special compensation scheme for the victims of crime is the need of hour.

India

In India, at present there is no comprehensive legislation except in the field of motor or factory accident for compensation to victims of crime. Only existing provision regarding payment of compensation to the victims is contained in the section 357 of CrPC. It provides compensation for loss or injury, caused by the criminal offence to the victim, after fine is imposed by the court. It is however, not mandatory for the state to pay compensation to the victims of crime. Compensation can also be awarded only if the offender is convicted of the offence with which he is charged. The amount of compensation is not uniform. It varies from case to case. However, Section 357(3) of CrPC, provides payment of compensation, even if fine does not form part of the punishment. The amount of compensation the court can order is flexible enough to make it truly compensatory. In Hari Kishan and State of Haryana versus Sukhbir Singh (AIR 1988 SC 2127), the court observed that, section 357 (3) is an important provision but the courts have seldom invoked it, perhaps due to ignorance of its objective. "*The power of the court to award compensation is not ancillary to other sentence, but it is in addition thereto. It is a measure of responding appropriately to crime as well as reconciling the victim with the offender. It is indeed a step forward in our criminal justice system. We therefore, recommended to all courts to exercise this power liberally so as to meet the ends of justice in a better way*".

The 47th Report of Law Commission regretted that the courts do not exercise the statutory power as freely and liberally as could be desired. It also recommended the insertion of a clause in Indian Penal Code, requiring the trial court to pass compensatory order, payable out of the fine imposed on the victims of crime. It also suggested an amendment of section 357 of CrPC to make obligatory for courts to record reasons for not doing so in suitable cases. However, these suggestions did not find favour with the lawmakers.

In 1992, the government of UP through an amendment to section 357 of CrPC provided that where the victim is a member of the Scheduled Caste or Scheduled Tribe and the person convicted is not such a member, then it shall be obligatory for the court to order compensation to the victims of crime. The person, who fails to pay the compensation, is normally required to undergo imprisonment, in default of the said payment. However, there are many instances of default and the victims have suffered in consequence.

Sympathizing with the plight of victims under the Criminal Justice Administration, the Supreme Court and High Courts in India, have evolved the practice of awarding compensatory remedies. The apex court's decisions in Nilabati Behera versus State of Orissa {(1993) 2 SCC, 746} and Chairman Board versus Chandrima Das {(2000) 2 SCC 465}, are illustrative of this new trend of using constitutional jurisdictions to do justice to the victims of crime. In 1985, the Indian Society of Victimology based in Chennai, prepared a Bill for Victim Compensation and submitted it to the government of India. No follow up action so far has been taken on this. Malimath committee, in its report *"Reform in the Criminal Justice System"* has suggested that it is an appropriate draft for initiating further action.

References

1. D. J. Hall, (1991) Victim Voices in Criminal Court: The Need for Restraint, American Criminal Law Review, 28, pp. 233-66).
2. V.N. Rajan, (1981) Victimology in India: An Introductory Study, pp.15-16.

24

Judicial Accountability

Sometime back, the judges of the Punjab and Haryana High Court proceeded on mass casual leave after a spat with the Chief Justice of the High Court. The unseemly episode was triggered by the action of the Chief Justice of Punjab and the Haryana High Court, issuing notices to two judges for accepting free membership of a club that was embroiled in litigation. The spectacle of judges going on a flash strike is unprecedented and has undoubtedly lowered the image of the judiciary. Of the three branches of the state, it is the judiciary, that is still held in high esteem. Unfortunately, danger to the integrity of the judicial system comes from within and not from outside. Bad appointments, poor supervision, unattractive salaries, absence of any process of weeding out the bad hats, have taken their toll. But what can be done to pull up the errant judges and ensure judicial accountability? 'Judicial credibility is enhanced,' says the Report of the Malimath Committee on Reforms of the Criminal Justice System, 'only when it is transparent and accountable'.

The Indian constitution guarantees independence of the judiciary, but at the same time, the judiciary remains subject to the rule of law, as anybody else. Article 225 of the Constitution gives High Court the power of control over sub-ordinate courts. If this power is properly exercised, accountability of the subordinate courts can be ensured. Unfortunately, this has not happened. Corruption in subordinate courts has now become a matter of public concern. As early as in 1962, the Santhanam Committee, which made a path-breaking study of the problems of corruption in the country reported that, 'Corruption exists in the lower ranks of the judiciary all over, and in some places, it has spread to the higher ranks also'.

However, as far as the High Courts are concerned, there is no power of control to be exercised by anyone over them, not even the Supreme Court. The High Courts, in that sense are independent, though their judgements can be reviewed by the Supreme Court. Some time back, a former Chief Justice of the Supreme Court bemoaned the lack of integrity among certain percentage of the judges of the High Courts and mentioned the difficulties of disciplining them.

Article 124 (4) of the Indian Constitution provides that a judge of the High Court or Supreme Court can be removed from office by the President for 'proved misbehavior or incapacity' after an address in each house of Parliament supported by a majority of the total membership of the House and by majority of not less than two thirds of the members of the House present and voting on the motion for the removal of the judge. In post-independence India, there has been only one impeachment motion in 1993 against Justice V. Ramasamy, a Supreme Court Judge. The impeachment motion failed, even though the enquiry committee had held that serious charges of misconduct were proved against the judge warranting his removal.

Some recent incidents of reportedly serious misconduct of some of the judges of the High Courts have shaken public confidence and given rise to a growing feeling among the public that if the judges are guilty of serious misconduct, nothing can be done about it. It is imperative that without undermining its independence, the judiciary itself has to take some meaningful steps to set its house in order and come forward with some credible solutions. It has to devise a system of judicial accountability that will protect the higher judiciary from some of its errant members. The ancient Latin adage 'Ne vibe jano justicia' (nothing should defile the temple of justice) has to be kept in mind.

Position Of The Chief Justice

Today, in the High Courts, the Chief Justice is regarded only as first among the equals and does not exercise any real control or authority over his colleagues. This has gone to erode discipline, which is absolutely necessary for efficient functioning of the institution. The Malimath Committee, in its report, has mentioned about judges not attending courts punctually, reserving judgements for long periods and acting vindictively against some lawyers. The Chief Justice has no power to look into these complaints and feels helpless. If the Chief Justice is empowered to look into such cases and take prompt corrective measures, many of these problems will be nipped in the bud. The Chief Justice should be authorized and empowered to take corrective measures like :

1. Censure the judges;
2. Withdraw the judicial work from the judge for a specified period;
3. Advise the judge to seek transfer or voluntary retirement and
4. Disabling the judge to hear a particular class of cases or in which a particular lawyer appears.

If these measures do not prove adequate or effective, the Chief Justice of the High Court also should have the power to move the Chief Justice of India, who should have the power to transfer the aberrant judge or move for his impeachment.

In USA, which faced similar problems because the judges can be removed only through impeachment process, enacted in 1980, the Judicial Councils Reform and Judicial Conduct and Disability. Under the Act, there is a judicial council for each circuit and the National Judicial Conference at the Apex. They have been given powers to censure a judge, requesting him to seek retirement or direct that no cases can be assigned to a judge for a limited period. Under this law, a committee of fellow judges investigated complaints against a Federal District Judge, John McBryde. He was reprimanded and suspended from hearing new cases for a year. McBryde took the plea that one year's suspension from hearing new cases was nothing, but temporary impeachment tantamounted to violation of judicial independence guaranteed by the US Constitution. His pleas were rejected and the US Supreme Court accepted the argument of the Solicitor General that the judicial independence protected by article III of the Constitution was meant to insulate judges from interference from other branches of the government and not from oversight by other judges.

It bears mention in this connection that for enforcing judicial accountability, the Supreme Court adopted in May, 1997, a code of conduct for judges styled as 'Restatement of values of Judicial Life'. Another resolution required a declaration of assets to be made by the Chief Justice and judges of the Supreme Court and High Courts. The resolution of the Supreme Court could furnish the basis for much needed legislative action, with necessary constitutional amendments. However, in trying to ensure judicial accountability, utmost care is to be taken to ensure that its independence is not diluted.

Further, the present system of dealing with complaints of misconduct against the judges is shrouded in secrecy and contempt laws hang like a sword of Damocles. The Contempt of Courts Act, 1971, prohibits exposures that would 'scandalize' the court. The Contempt of Courts Act does not say that truth cannot be a defence and it is for the Courts to interpret the meaning of the word 'scandalize'. But truth can never scandalize. Justice MN Venkatachliah, the former Chairman, National Human Rights Commission and former Chief Justice of Supreme Court, was fond of quoting the saying of American Judge Louis D Brandies that 'sunlight is the best disinfectant' and 'electric light is the most efficient policeman'.

Judicial probity is also closely linked with proper appointment of judges in the higher courts. Health of the judiciary will be judged by the quality of people appointed as judges. For instilling respect for the judiciary in public mind, it is necessary that persons of high level of integrity and professional competence are appointed as High Court and Supreme Court judges. The previous system of judicial appointment by the executive (1950-93) in consultation with the judiciary was substituted by a judicial collegium of five senior judges. Now the question of setting up of a National Judicial Commission to deal with the appointment of judges is under active consideration. But mere change of institutional mechanism will not help. No system can be ultimately better than those who operate it. A transparent procedure of selection has to be devised, so as to ensure appointment of judges of integrity commanding public confidence. The Malimath Committee recommended that a set of guidelines should be evolved laying down relevant qualifications, attributes, character and integrity that are necessary to be a good judge and indicate the evidence or materials from which these can be inferred. This may ensure that irrelevant considerations or favouritism do not substantially influence appointments of the judges.

25

Human Rights in 21st Century

Twentieth Century stands out as the century that witnessed remarkable advancement as well as abject denial of human rights. In 1948, when the Universal Declaration of Human Rights was adopted as *"a common standard of achievement of all peoples and nations"*, there were reservations of many state governments. Virtually all states shielded behind Article 2 (7) of the UN Charter arguing that human rights matter was strictly an internal matter of the states concerned. Due to reservation of state governments, the Universal Declaration of Human Rights, was not presented to the General Assembly as a treaty for ratification, which would be binding upon the signatory nations, but an instrument to be endorsed as *"a statement of goals and aspirations – a vision of the world as the International community wanted it to be become"*. The Declaration was adopted by an affirmative vote of 48 member states and 8 abstentions. While a UN Commission on Human Rights was set up, its work was entirely dominated by the governments and the role of NGOs was restricted to adhoc appearances. The commission's mandate was confined in practice to the drafting of new treaties and other legal instruments.

However, before the twentieth century came to an end, there were many remarkable and important developments in the domain of human rights. The view that human rights violations are essentially domestic rights matter receives now very little credence from the International Community. The Universal Declaration has been supplemented by a vast array of international standards; the most important of which are the *six "core"* human Rights treaties. The UN has also created a vast array of monitoring mechanisms.

Human Rights And Democracy

One of the important advancements of the twentieth century was the recognition of democracy as, to quote Amartya Sen, "*preeminently acceptable form of governance*". Though democracy is not the only means by which improved governance could be achieved, it is perhaps the only reliable one. By providing greater public participation, democracy enhances the likelihood that national developmental goals will reflect broad societal aspirations and priorities. By establishing political legitimacy of governments, democracy strengthens their capacity to function efficiently and effectively. Thus, human rights and democracy are mutually supportive.

However, history is not linear. Twentieth century also witnessed some of the worst instances of human rights violations. Only six years before the century ended, more than half a million citizens of Rwanda were murdered by their government in a state sponsored genocide. It was expected that the end of the cold war, which saw the downfall of many totalitarian regimes, would bring about improvements in respect of human rights. It was hoped that post-cold war increase in democracy would lead to human rights advancement. However, it was found, as Helen Fein[1] pointed out "there had been more murder in the middle". This means that life integrity violations are more likely to occur in societies that lie between democracy and authoritarianism. The democratization of authoritarian political systems has sometimes proved dangerous for protection of human rights.

Nineties of twentieth century also saw that in different circumstances, gross local human rights violations have catalyzed military action by outside agents acting on authority of multi national bodies. UN Secretary General, Kofi Annan, called for systematic doctorine of UN Human rights intervention. He has said that *"the world cannot stand aside when gross systemic violations of human rights are taking place."*

Globalisation

As human society enters twenty first century, the unfortunate fact that stares us in the face is that global gap between haves and have-nots has widened. Globalization has led to growing marginalization of poor nations and growing human insecurity and inequality. UN Human Development Report, 1999, tersely comments *"the benefits of globalization in the past decades have been so unevenly shared that the very word has come to acquire in certain quarters a pejorative tinge."*

Calling globalization as the central challenge to be faced today, the world leaders attending the UN Millennium Summit on 8th September, 2000, stated that while globalization offers great opportunities, at present it benefits are unevenly distributed. With globalization and emergence of powerful Multi National Corporations, (MNCs) the role of the governments is diminishing and they are relinquishing their responsibilities of serving the needs of those citizens, who are unable to protect themselves.

Role of NGOs

Another important development in the field of human rights is the increasingly important role of Non-Governmental Organisations (NGOs). They have done useful work in popularizing the ideas and concepts of human rights and drawing attention of international agencies to egregious violations of human rights in different quarters of the globe. NGOs have also encouraged the growth of human rights culture that cuts across national political boundaries. They constitute, to use the evocative phrase of Elenaor Roosevelt "*a curious grape vine*". Their functions include education, advocacy, standard setting, monitoring and in some cases enforcement. UN human rights institutions were suspicious of the NGOs at first, but gradually made increasing use of them. NGOs also play and will continue to play, an important role in international conferences. Amnesty International's fight for abolition of death penalty, the role of Habitat International Coalition and other NGOs to get Istanbul Declaration of Acceptance of Human Right of Housing are some of the landmark contributions of NGO groups. Increase in the number of NGOs is, however, causing problems of cooperation. There is now some tension between western based NGOs, which are well established and well resourced and the NGOs from poorer countries, which are less resourced and have different perspectives on human rights.

National Institutions

National institutions in different countries have come up and become effective fora and instruments for promotion and protection of human rights, particularly, in the areas of combating racism, racial discrimination and ethnic violence, etc. One of the important items in the human rights agenda of 21st century will be to strengthen the national institutions and set up such institutions in states, where they do not exist. NGOs and National institutions complement one another and working together, can constitute effective instruments for advancement of human rights. In India, constitution of National Human Rights Commission and State Human Rights Commissions, have been important milestones in the onward movement of human rights.

Gender Equality

Women continue to be discriminated all over the world and are subject to many forms of violence. Inspite of ratification of regional and International Instruments, many states still maintain laws and practices, which discriminate against women. Selective practices and customs used by states, perpetuate discrimination. This is particularly true in the field of access to land and other important economic resources and rights within the family. Crimes against women, which are increasing exponentially, are crimes against humanity and failure of the governments to prosecute those, who are responsible for such crimes, imply complicity.

The Report on "Human Development in South Asia, 2000", dealing with gender question focuses on deprivation borne by women in South Asia. In the foreword, Mahabub-ul-Haq aptly remarks "*as we approach the 21 century, we hear quiet steps of rising revolution for gender equality. Women have greatly expanded their capabilities over last few decades through liberal investment in their education. It is quite clear, that the 21 century will be the century of much greater gender equality than the world has seen so far.*"

Terrorism

Terrorism will continue to pose another serious threat to human rights in the coming decades. Successive resolutions of United Nation's General Assembly and United Nations Commission for Human Rights have stated that terrorism in all its forms and manifestations, whenever and by whomsoever committed, can never be justified. There is need for international community to enhance cooperation in order to fight against terrorism in accordance with relevant international instruments including those relating to human rights. Terrorist violence has to be combated, but it has to be fought in a manner that accords due respect to human rights, whatever the difficulties it may entail for the state and all those engaged in the task.

UN Secretary General Kofi Annan, has aptly said "A genocide begins with the killing of one man not for what he has done but because of who he is. A campaign of ethnic cleansing begins with one nation turning on another. Poverty begins when one child is denied his/her fundamental rights to education. Indeed what begins as a failure to uphold the dignity of one life, all too often ends as calamity for the entire nation."

Universality

The issue of universality of human rights will continue to trigger debates and divisions in this new century. Many Asian countries, which are parties to the UN Charter and signatories to Universal Declaration feel that western countries are utilizing human rights institutions for their own ends and ideological hegemony. The nub of Asian criticism is that the western concept of human rights is a western imposition, an act of moral and cultural imperialism. There is criticism that developed countries are seeking to impose western values on non-western societies under the guise of promoting good governance and human rights. The Vienna Declaration, 1993, tried to set at rest the debate between the primacy of civil and political rights on one hand and social and economic rights on the other. It categorically stated that human rights are interdependent, interrelated and universal. However, in the Vienna Conference, the head of the Chinese delegate categorically stated "one should not and cannot think of human rights standards and morals of certain countries as the only proper one and demand all countries comply with them. It is neither realistic nor workable to make international economic assistance or even international cooperation conditional on them."

It is true that protection of social and economic rights compared to protection of civil and political rights at both national and international level have been poor and irregular. Very often, social and economic rights are considered aspirational and non-justiciable. There is also fallacious thinking that negative rights, which gather round our own liberties, are more important than positive rights, that evolve from our basic needs. The argument that one set of rights is prerequisite for enjoyment of other sets of rights, is self-serving and fallacious. They are also without any legal and empirical foundations and destroy the basis of an international human rights consciousness. In the 21st century, there must be holistic and integrated approach of human rights and one set of rights cannot be bargained for the other.

POVERTY

In today's world, nearly three quarters of humanity, who live in developing countries of Asia, Africa and Latin America, are weighed down by poverty and underdevelopment. Widespread poverty among the masses in the developing countries is a great cause of denial of human rights. Poverty destroys human dignity and without human dignity, there can be no human rights or the capacity to fight against the denial of human rights. In these societies, there are massive violations of human rights of disadvantaged groups and marginalized sections of the society. State often is the major culprit but in many instances civil society, which is feudal in its outlook and approach, is the perpetrator of these violations, with the connivance of state administration.

It has to be borne in mind that the problems of human rights in the countries of Asian and Africa are quite different from those in the west. In western countries, the role of human rights is to fine-tune the administrative and judicial system and fortify the rights and freedoms that are largely uncontroversial. But in developing countries, human rights have a transformative potential. They are a constant challenge to the vested interests in society, riven by enormous disparity of wealth and power with traditions of authoritarianism and helplessness of disadvantaged communities[2].

It is therefore, imperative to strengthen movements for implementation of human rights in developing countries. For effective implementation of human rights, what is needed is a strong sensitive human rights conscience, which acts on the belief that human rights are indivisible and their protection is the abiding responsibility of civilized international community. Human rights conscientisation should be the first item in the agenda of successful human rights movement in 21st century.

References

1. Fein H. (1005) – More Murders in the Middle Life Integrity Violations and Democracy in the World (1987).
2. Yash Ghai "Asian Perspective on Human Rights".

26

Scourge of Dowry Violence

The National Commission for Women has suggested a number of amendments to the Dowry Prohibition Act, 1961, to provide more teeth in it. It has asked the government to remove the restriction of seven years in the law for booking a person under the Act. The Commission's Chairperson has said that there are many cases, where dowry has been demanded from the women's family even 25/30 years after the marriage. The proposed amendment will provide relief to such women. The NCW has further proposed that the victim or her family should have the right to claim gifts received during the wedding, in addition to existing provisions of seeking *"Stree Dhan"*. In a 1985 judgment, the Supreme Court held that *"stree dhan"*, that is any property given to the wife in the form of jewellery and other assets, is an absolute property and her husband and in-laws are bound to return it, if she demands the property. (Pratibha Rani vs Suraj Kumar, AIR 1985 SC 628). A list of gifts received in the marriage will be prepared and vetted by the Protection officers to be appointed, as per the proposal. There will be appointment of service officers and protection officers similar to the one under Domestic Violence Act. NCW's proposal also wants to make the bride's parents liable for paying dowry. Parents will have to submit a proof of their income like income-tax return, while claiming the amount of dowry given. This will, as the Chairperson of NCW claims, prevent some fraudulent claims under 498A IPC.

The proposal of NCW, now reportedly accepted by the government, has been criticized by some legal experts on the ground that the contemplated anti-dowry provisions will be draconian and will result in making marriage an overly legalistic affair. Earlier, when Justice J.D. Kapoor of Delhi High Court stated in a case that anti-dowry prohibitions in Indian Penal Code were being misused and such misuse is undermining the institution of marriage and proving detrimental to the health of the society, his observations were decried by some women's organizations as reflection of *"judiciary's male chauvinistic attitude."*

It is a hard fact that cancerous evil of dowry has spread like an epidemic. It is not confined to a particular community but has permeated to other communities, which were earlier traditionally averse to accepting dowry. A couple of decades back, dowry was practically unknown in most parts of Assam. But a survey conducted by the All India Democratic Women's Association in 2003 in five districts of Assam showed that dowry system has become common among the people of Assam. What is more distressing is that this evil practice is more evident among the educated and so-called respectable middle and lower middle classes. As the Director of the National police Academy, I had noted with distress how All India Service Officers shamelessly asked for heavy dowries throwing to the winds all other considerations. Even educated women silently suffer dowry torture and harassment. A survey conducted by the Centre of Social Research for the Ministry of Human Resources showed that 90% of dowry victims covered by the study were educated – 30% were graduates and 20% were working women contributing to the family income.

According to National Crimes Record Bureau (2005 figures), there had been 6787 dowry death cases in India under IPC and 3204 dowry harassment cases under the Dowry Prohibition Act 1961. Majority of the cases were reported from Bihar and Uttar Pradesh. But the statistics do not give a correct picture as a large number of cases are suppressed. A study done by the Institute of Development and Communication (IDC), showed that for every reported dowry violence case almost 229 cases go unreported and unregistered.

Though 94% of cruelty by husbands/relatives under section 498(a) and 304(b) IPC are charge sheeted by the police, conviction rates, however, in cases of offences u/s 498(a) are between 19-20% and in respect of offences u/s 304(b) is 32%.

A major study on reported unnatural deaths of 1000 married women in Punjab conducted by Dr DC Sharma of Punjab State Chemical Laboratory from 2002-2006, established clear linkages between the state's low sex ratio and the problem of dowry. Out of these 1000 cases of unnatural deaths of married women aged between 18-35 years, 176 related to dowry and in 84% of these dowry death cases, poisoning was the cause of death and not burning as is usually assumed. This is because of free availability of lethal insecticides in the agriculture sector. Because of the easy availability of pesticides in rural households accounted for 71% of total dowry deaths.

Though some stringent anti-dowry provisions are at times misused, the hard fact remains that these provisions of *law have remained more unused then misused*. The Dowry Prohibition Act was passed in 1961 but the passing of the act produced no tangible impact. Not a single case could be convicted under the Act till 1978. A new Act with more teeth was passed by the parliament – Criminal Law Amendments 1983 to deal with the problem. It inserted a new section in the Indian Penal Code, 498A to penalize the husband and the relatives of the husband, if they treat the woman in a cruel manner, for which she is forced to commit suicide. A new section, 113A was also inserted in the Indian Evidence Act to enable the court to presume that women have been tortured by the husband or relations of the husband to commit suicide if she committed suicide within a period of 7 years.

However, mere stiffening of the provisions of law will not help unless there is will to implement them vigorously. The Dowry Prohibition Amendment Act, 1986, enjoins the state government to appoint dowry prohibition officers u/s 8(b) with a hope that dowry prohibition officers would render assistance to persons subjected to dowry demands and help in collection of evidence and prosecution of the offenders. Unfortunately, dowry prohibition officers are not functioning in most of the states.

The Malimath Committee set up to reform the criminal justice system found fault with section 498(a) and recommended that the offence should be made bailable. Women's organizations have very rightly opposed any such softening of the provisions of law. There is no doubt that the provisions of 498(a) and 113(c) of Evidence Act have had a deterrent effect. This is our experience in the field.

Section 498(a) has been a valuable reform in the Indian context. I know of cases, when the husband and the in-laws have refrained from harassing the girl because of the fear that stringent provisions of law may be invoked. A phenomenal number of cases continue to be registered under this section. In 2004, 58121 cases were registered against 45788 in 2000, 49170 in 2001, 49237 in 2002, 50703 in 2003, and 58121 in 2004, marking an increase of 14.6 over that of the previous year. The statistics not only comment on the inability of the law to tackle the issue, but also reflect the existence of the problem, which prior to the amendment was so long swept under the carpet. Hence, some draconian provisions in anti-dowry laws are necessary. However, mere existence of laws will not prevent outrageous violation of human rights like dowry offences. Laws do not protect human rights only the people do. During the debate in the Parliament on dowry bill in 1961, Pandit Jawahar

Lal Nehru said, *"Legislation by itself cannot solve deep-seated social problems, but legislation is necessary and essential so that it may give the push and have that educative factor and legal sanctions behind it, which help public opinion to be given a certain shape."*

Nearly 100 years ago Ravindra Nath Tagore wrote a moving story "*Dena-Pwna*" in which the helpless heroine *Neru* was driven to death by cruel in-laws because the dowry her father has provided was considered inadequate. It is a crowing pity that the situation has not changed. The Hindu Succession Act 1956, providing for equal share of property to the daughters appears to have unintentionally contributed to the evils of the dowry system as the prospective in-laws instead of claiming the share by the daughter-in-law in her father's property after the marriage prefer to demand the same in the form of dowry at the time of marriage.

There is no real redress unless educated women stand up and fight their battles. Ultimately, effective resistance has to come from the girls and their parents, not after the abuse but before. Today anti-dowry movement is petering out in the country. A resolute campaign is necessary against this evil to stir the conscience of society and treat those, who have taken and given dowries as social pariahs. In the words of Mahatma Gandhi, "*acceptance of dowry is a disgrace for a young man who accepts it as well as a dishonor for women folk*". These words should ring in the ears of every unmarried young woman and man.

27

Illicit Organ Trade

It is reported in the press that the Union Ministry of Health and Family Welfare has proposed stringent amendments to the transplantation of Human Organs Act, 1994. The amendment seeks to enhance the punishment of the offenders under the Act and also put curbs on foreigners, who come to India for organ transplant. Until the passage of Organ Transplantation Act 1994, there was no legislation to prohibit the sale of organs. Poverty and economic hardship, coupled with the fact that donating a kidney is not very risky made India one of the largest centers for kidney transplantation in the world. Kidney transplantation operation sharply increased after drugs were developed in the 1970s to control body's rejection of foreign objects. The pace of demand for kidneys did not keep up with the supply. Consequently, large number of poor people sold kidneys for lure of money or forced to give up their kidney unknowingly. The World Health Organization (WHO) viewed the commercialization of human organs, as a 'violation of human rights and dignity' and enunciated a guiding principle, which states that 'the human body and its parts cannot be the subject of commercial transactions.'

Transplantation of Human Organs Act 1994 was enacted, to stop the illegal practice of organ sale. It illegalized buying and selling of human organs and declared cash for kidney transplants, a criminal offence. Under sec 19 of the Act, participation in or an abetment of organ trade, invites punishment with a term of imprisonment of 2 to 7 years. However, the Act proved to be ineffective and totally failed to achieve its objective. The Act makes the offence of kidney trading non-cognizable. In other words, the police cannot look into the complaints of kidney trading independently and must wait for a complaint to be made by the appropriate authority, set up under the Act or by an individual, who has given prior notice of not less then 60 days to the appropriate authority. The Act also permits a near relative, defined as a patient spouse, siblings or children to donate a kidney to the patient. Further, sec 9(3) of the Act allows donors, who are not near relatives but willing to donate kidneys to the recipients *"by reason of affection or attachment towards the recipient or for any special reasons"*. Sec 9(3), thus, deliberately provides a loophole, which turned out to be a fatal infirmity of the Act. It was exploited in practice by unscrupulous operators with a view to making moneysd out of the transaction. There was also utter failure of the authorization committee in many states to function effectively as a watchdog.

Punjab Kidney Transplant Scam

A senior police officer from the National Police Academy, Hyderabad, enquired into a series of illegal kidney transplant cases in the cities of Amritsar, Jalandhar and Chandigarh in 2004. It transpired that the key players of the kidney transplant were authorization committee members, lawyers, police officers, politicians, as well as the trained hospital staff. The kingpin was a senior nephrologist. The donors were mainly poor migrant labourers coming from different parts of the country to seek jobs in Punjab. Victims were recruited individually or in groups of 6 or 7 and shown as living with the recipients for past 8 to 15 years as domestic servants. After the transplantation, the donors were not kept in the hospital for proper post-operative care and were quickly discharged. Many of the donors lost physical strength due to lack of post-operative care and in some cases, some of the poor donors expired on the operation table.

As a legal requirement under sec 9(3) of the Act, the unrelated donor and the recipient have to file an affidavit in a magistrate's court, clearly stating that the donor is donating the kidney for reasons of "*affection and attachment towards the recipient*". Some selected advocates were part of the organized gang, who got the fake affidavits drafted and attested. The authorization committee were supposed to hold a mandatory enquiry under sec 9(5) of the Act and only after satisfying itself with the full compliance and requirements of the Act, it could grant approval and allow transplant of the human organs. The committee, however, approved cases without even bothering to make a preliminary enquiry from the donors. During police investigation, a former member of the authorization committee gave a statement in the court that he had opposed various malpractices regarding kidney donations in unrelated cases but in vain. The Chairman and members of the committee were in league with the main accused and the middlemen and overruled him.

Recently, in some cases of kidney transplant, the Delhi police had accused the authorization committee of Army Research and Referral Hospital, which sanctions permission for organ transplant, of negligence while giving sanctions and charge sheeted some of the employees of the hospital for being involved in a number of illegal transplant cases that took place at the hospital.

In the recent sensational case of kidney kingpin Amit Kumar, it came to light that he had conducted nearly 500 kidney transplants in his clinic at Gurgaon. There was clear collusion between the medical community and the organ traffickers. Amit, a quack, conducted kidney transplant operations without the help of qualified surgeons and had built up an international network for attracting recipients. However, the hard fact to be contended with is that the unequal march of demand and supply of kidneys has created a huge black market in India. It is estimated that 5000 or more kidneys are sold every year in the country. It is reported that the lucrative trade has touched the turnover of approximately Rs 150 crore each year. Many doctors are also worried about the long term consequences of these activities. They point out that a number of HIV Positive patients are trying to sell their kidneys to earn a living.

For combating the problem, mere tightening of legal provisions alone will not suffice. There is need for upgrading the skill of law enforcement officers in respect of organ trafficking related investigations. Authorization committees, which have proved to be a part of the problem and not solution, should be revamped. They should have respected members of the civil society, besides health professionals, to act as effective watchdogs. There is also need for strongly campaigning for more cadaver transplants. There should be rethinking on organ retrieval after death. Government can examine and standardize the procedures of some of the NGOs, who have attained notable successes in organ retrieval.

28

Decriminalization of Homosexuality

Union Ministries of Health and Home are at loggerheads over the issue of decriminalization of homosexuality. The Health Ministry wants Section 377 of the Indian Penal Code, which criminalizes homosexuality, to be deleted on the ground that it is impeding the country's fight against HIV. The Home Ministry, however, wants the penal provisions to be retained as its deletion would encourage delinquent behaviour. The Health Minister, Ramadoss, is of the firm view that homosexuality should be decriminalized, especially, from the point of health issues; the children, however, should be protected against sexual abuse and paedophiles treated as criminals. The Prime Minister has now directed both the Home Minister and the Health Minister to discuss the matter and sort out the differences.

Section 377, which criminalizes homosexuality was introduced by Lord MaCaulay as a part of the Indian Penal Code in 1860. It punishes "*carnal intercourse against the order of nature*" with imprisonment of ten years or life, or with fine. Section 377 of the Penal Code defines unnatural offences as 'whosoever voluntarily has carnal intercourse against the order of nature with any man, woman or animal, shall be punished with imprisonment for life, or with imprisonment of either description for a term which may extend to ten years and shall also be liable to fine.

Ironically, Section 377 of the IPC, replaces a tolerant Indian attitude towards the homosexuals with a highly oppressive one. There is nothing in Indian scriptures whether Hindu, Muslim, Buddhist, Jain, that refers to homosexuality as *'taboo'* and forbidden. This outdated law violates the fundamental rights of the homosexuals and under the law even any consensual sex is branded as sodomy and the people can be booked. Section 377 of the Indian Penal Code and its identical twins in Bangladesh, Malaysia, Singapore and other former colonies was, a British imperial law meant for export and not domestic consumption. Anti-homo British domestic law is derived from *"gross indecency"* amendment at the end of the nineteenth century. The law was used against Oscar Wilde. However, it was found in UK, that the law was being unfairly used for blackmailing people. In England, homosexual behaviour between consenting adults was decriminalized in 1967, pursuant to the Wolfenden Committee Report. In 1981, Jeffery Dudgeon, a shipping clerk in Belfast and a gay rights activist, applied to the European Court of Human Rights, challenging the provisions outlawing homosexuality in Northern Ireland on the ground that they violated his privacy rights under Article 8 and the Right to Equality and Non-discrimination under Article 14 of the European Convention of Human Rights. The Court declared the law, insofar as it criminalized homosexual acts between consenting adults in private, as impinging on the privacy right under Article 8, but did not consider necessary to deal with the equality challenge.

In the United Kingdom, interesting cases arose from the Government's absolute policy of banning employment of homosexuals in the Armed Forces. In the case of one Duncon Lustig-Orean, the Royal Navy terminated his services on the ground of sexual orientation. He failed in the High Court and the House of Lords. The European Court, while affirming the right of every State to formulate its own policy regarding the Armed Forces, held that on the facts of the case, his privacy right was violated and the Government was unable to justify its absolute policy with concrete evidence and to substantiate its allegations of negative effects on the Armed Forces. He was awarded substantial pecuniary damages.

The South African Constitution of 1996, has a unique provision in its Bill of Rights. Article 9 provides equality before the law and enjoins the State as well as all persons not to discriminate, directly or indirectly, against anyone on several grounds, including sexual orientation. The Hongkong Court of Appeal in September, 2006, unanimously invalidated similar provisions in Hongkong laws, which criminalize homosexual practices in private between consenting adults. It is worth recalling that Justice Michel Kirby, one of the distinguished serving judges of the High Court of Australia and Justice Edwin Cameron, now a serving judge of Supreme Court of South Africa, have publicly acknowledged their gay status for many years.

Although prosecutions under Section 377 of the Indian Penal Code are few, the fact remains that it has been used to harass those with alternative sexual orientation and also remains an intolerant symbol of the unacceptability of the gay behaviour. The Naz Foundation, a Delhi-based NGO, has now filed a public interest litigation before the Delhi High Court. It is not seeking the repeal of Section 377 it is only asking for it to be 'read down' in a manner that stops it from being applied to consensual sex between adults'. The Section can be used for penalizing non-consensual sex and child sex abuse. The Delhi High Court now has pulled up the Union Government for terming homosexual trait as a disease. But there are experts holding different views. American Psychological Association has opined that homosexuality is no longer viewed by mental health professionals as a disease or disorder. "*Homosexual orientation may well form part of the very fiber of an individual's personality.*"

Two years ago, prominent citizens of the country came forward to endorse a letter signed by author Vikram Seth for decriminalizing homosexuality. The signatories, included economist Amratya Sen, author Arundhuty Roy, social activist Swami Agnivesh and others. The letter says, 'It is surprising that independent India has not been able to rescind the colonial era monstrosity, in the shape of Section 377, dating from 1861. That, as it happens, was the year in which the American Civil War began, which would ultimately abolish the unfreedom of slavery in America. Today, 145 years later, we surely have urgent reason to abolish in India, with our commitment to democracy and human rights, the unfreedom of arbitrary and unjust criminalization.'

Today, homosexuality is recognized across the globe, with Netherlands being the first country to permit marriage between gay couples. The UK has also passed legislation recognizing gay relationships. But unfortunately in India, as the sociologist Radhika Chopra puts it, *"Overt emphasis on reproduction has made same sex love a taboo. Our law must march in step with times"*. The need for reform is urgent, because Section 377 poses a threat to public health by impeding programmes for prevention and control of HIV/AIDS.

Section 377 also violates human rights standards, including, provisions of the Indian Constitution, on equality and non-discrimination. Awareness among the media, law enforcement officers, judiciary and the intelligentsia, has to be raised regarding social intolerance fostered by the legal regime of Section 377 and how it entails violation of human rights.

In 1998, the Constitutional Court of South Africa, unanimously invalidated provisions of several criminal laws, which made homosexual conduct punishable between consenting adults as violative of Equality Clause. This judgment was delivered on application of the National Coalition for Gay and Lesbian Equality and the South African Human Rights Commission. The Court observed that even though the provisions in South African law against homosexual practices were not enforced, the provisions were invalidated, because they reduced gays to the "*status of unapprehended felons*", thus entrenching stigma and encouraging discrimination."

29

Noble Cause Corruption

"Noble cause corruption" entered the literature with Edwin Delattre's influential book *"Character and Cops: Ethics in Policing"*, first published in 1989. It has now become a standard phrase for characterizing behaviour in which, in order to achieve apparently legitimate objectives, the police exceed their authority and powers. The concept has classical origin. In Plato's *"Republic"* the philosopher King, justifies the use of noble lies, in order to advance the good of the city. But whereas for Plato, the noble cause does not justify anything more than the use of lies and other forms of deception. Police often engaged in *"noble cause justification indulge in misuse of force and other forms of flagrant abuse of human rights."*

At first blush, noble cause corruption differs in many ways from what is generally referred as corruption. Noble corruption in policing is defined as corruption committed in the name of good ends; corruption that happens, when police officers care too much about their own work and corruption committed in order to get the bad guys off the streets.

Police corruption has been traditionally defined as misuse of authority by an officer for personal gain and accepting money or money's worth to provide a service that the police are duty-bound to provide. Many police officers feel that corruption for personnel gain is much more serious than engaging in corrupt behaviour that tends to benefit the society at large.

Dirty Harry Problem

The notion of noble cause corruption receives classic expression in Dirty Harry Film and its chief protagonist, anti-hero Inspector Harry. In this, detective Harry Callaghan is trying to achieve a good end. He is trying to find out a girl, whose life is in imminent danger. In order to save the girl, he is inflicting pain and torture upon the kidnapper, who is refusing to reveal her whereabouts. The image of Harry Callaghan inflicting pain upon a psychopath, is emotionally compelling. But in most of the instances, police either fabricate evidence or use excessive force not for saving the life of the victim, nor are they proved to be the only means of conviction. Such high-handed methods not only violate the right of the suspect, but also affect the moral fibre of the policemen indulging in such methods. They view their dirty acts, not as means to the achievement of good ends but as ends in themselves. It is also a fact that corrupt acts, including, acts of noble cause corruption, are habitual action. They are not one-off immoral action committed for good ends. Very often, the motivating force is the habit and disposition on the part of the police officers, to commit such acts. There is no attempt to perform a rational calculation of the morality of ends and means on a case by case basis.

Ends and Means

Noble cause corruption implies faith in the concept that *the end justifies the means*. However, in the conflict of ends and means, the point to be borne in mind is that, if the ends are important enough to justify the means. The conviction of a criminal is important but in a liberal democracy, the police are expected to carry out anti crime activities in a manner that advances the values of a liberal democratic society. Ends, therefore, have to be important enough to serve the justificatory function. Adoption of impermissible means may ultimately undermine the end.

Again many means have some other consequences that perhaps may make their use inappropriate. In post 9/11 world, to curb terrorism, draconian laws have been passed in many democratic countries but enforcement and misuse of laws in many democratic countries, including India, shows that some ways of keeping a country secure for freedom, may have the effect of diminishing as well as jeopardizing the other values of a democratic society.

Some justify torture to fight terrorism. It has been argued that torture is justified in some rare cases. In America, the most significant exponent of this position is Alan Dreshweitz, a leading criminal defence lawyer, who has argued that in cases of "*ticking bomb urgency*", torture warrants may be issued. In practice, however, attempts to use torture sparingly have led to widespread abuse. Once a degree of torture is permitted, it gives the licence to the interrogators to use it systematically and abusively. The argument that enemies deserve no justice, will lead to deterioration of justice for all.

Again the issue of proportionality of the means has to be kept in view. Otherwise, legitimate means will be judged inappropriate, if the aims are not considered of sufficient importance to sustain their use. Along with the principle of proportionality, one has to keep in mind "*the principle of least restrictive alternative*". Even if the use of force is justified to realize a certain end, there is a need to adopt least restrictive tactics.

Systematic Arrogance

It is often seen that corruption, and particularly, noble cause corruption, occurs in a climate of arrogance, which generates a belief that police officers know what is best for the society and have the right to use power and influence to punish anyone posing, according to their perception, threats to public order and public safety. But arrogance, indeed, has no place in policing and an agency with a culture of arrogance will only foster allegations of organisational tolerance for noble cause corruption. Again supervisory cowardice has the effect of encouraging organisational tolerance of noble cause corruption. Unless senior officers take a resolute stand against various forms of misconduct of the subordinates illegal, practices and patterns will continue.

One popular and common form of noble cause corruption is testimonial deception, for ensuring conviction of someone believed to be guilty of criminal activity. Such deceptions can take various forms – fabrication of material evidence, selective presentation of evidence and improper collusion in the presentation of evidence, etc. Very often, such deceptions amount to perjury. According to Jeremy Booth, "*noble cause corruption is an elegant term for securing conviction on evidence that has been improved by the police. It is a euphemism for perjury.*"

Dirty Hands

Writers like Michael Walzer, hold the view that political leaders, police and military personnel have to engage in some form of noble cause corruption, which is a definitive feature of their roles. They have "*dirty hands*" as they have to perform actions, which infringe on the principles of morality. But some of the steps they are forced to take may be morally justified, though they involve use of apparently questionable methods. According to Walzer, politicians get their hands dirty and in his influential article on the topic offers examples. He gives the example of a political leader, who must order the torture a terrorist chief, with a view to discovering the whereabouts of a bomb, likely to kill innocent people. But this is an exceptional situation that does not occur routinely. This is an unusual emergency, when moral principles can be infringed for the sake of greater public good.

Writers like Delattre are of the view that in such hard and difficult cases, where there is conflict between ends and means, responsibility for any such decision should rest with the person with greater authority in the police department. Some procedural constraints should be placed on such decision making. The people, who are paid more and have greater expertise, must take greater responsibility. But in fast moving and difficult policing work, this kind of referral may not always be possible. In police work, important decisions affecting life and liberties of people have often to be taken by street patrolling officers and men down the line. They have to be vested with enormous discretion. It is aptly said that the command and control system of police organisation is paradoxical. It seems to regulate in minute ways the behaviour of the individuals, who are required by the nature of their work, to make instant and complex decisions in unpredictable circumstances. Police organisations allow enormous discretion in practice, while at the same time, maintain a top-down command system.

There is great need for training of police officers and men, in humane and ethical policing. The police have to develop sensitivity for those, who are policed, both suspects and victims. In policing, mechanical application of rules do not always help. Officers have to use their discretion. Discretion is not license. Though grounded on rules, discretion is a form of judgement, rather than mere rule following.

30

Corruption and Development

The World Bank has defined corruption as *"the use of public office for private good"*. In its widest connotation, corruption includes improper or selfish use of power or influence, attached to a public office or to a special position, one occupies in public life. Corruption is a complex phenomenon and in one form or other, has always existed. In India, as early as in 4th century BC, Kautilya (Minister of Indian emperor Chandra Gupta Maurya) in his famous *Arthasastra*[1] refers to various forms of corruption, prevalent in his time. He writes *"just as it is impossible, not to taste the honey, or the poison that finds itself at the tip of the tongue, so it is impossible for a government servant, not to eat up or at least a bit of king's revenue. Just as fish moving underwater, cannot possibly be found either drinking or not drinking water, so government servants employed in the government work, cannot be found out taking money for themselves."*

However, with the advent of globalization the problem of corruption has acquired transnational dimensions and is posing serious challenges for developing countries, suffering from weak institutions and lack of resources.

Speed Money

Some writers have argued that corruption and bribery are necessary lubricants, for a cumbersome system of administration. It enables entrepreneurs to bypass irksome and stultifying regulations and helps the process of development. Samual P Huntington[2] has bluntly stated that, in terms of economic growth, the only thing worse than a rigid, over-centralized, dishonest bureaucracy is a rigid, over-centralized, honest bureaucracy. It has also been argued, that corruption can have a desirable distributive impact, as it shifts income and wealth from richer individuals and companies to poorer ones. These arguments, however, do not stand the glare of serious scrutiny. Speed money often in practice, slows down the wheels of administration. Corruption, even when it is petty and routine, can not be a means of stimulating economic growth and improving living standards. It causes illegal transfer of state revenue to richer individuals, who are in a position to pay bribes, to the detriment of those who are not. Available empirical evidence shows, positive relationship between the extent of bribery and the amount of time, that enterprise managers spend with the officials. World Economic Forum Global Competitiveness Survey for 1997, surveyed 59 countries and obtained responses from 3000 firms showing that, enterprises reporting greater incidence of bribery also tend to spend a greater share of management time with bureaucrats and public officials regarding licenses, permits and taxes[3].

Anti-development

Corruption jeopardizes development in several ways. First, it distorts public spending. Distortion arises by deflecting allotted resources, from their original purpose. Public resources are deflected in corrupt regimes, because allocation goes where corrupt officials and politicians gain most. Contracts are awarded in a nepotic fashion, rather than on the basis of merit. Poor people become the primary victims of corruption, as they are denied services, because the resources are directed elsewhere. Second, corruption undermines efficiency Public sector efficiency suffers because, corruption imposes informal practices over proper views and procedures of the government. It also adds direct and indirect costs to the execution of the programmes. A 1996 survey showed that, within Ukraine, firm owners who pay large sums of bribes, had to spend one third more time with officials than firm owners who pay less bribes[4].

Third, corruption also saps economic growth. In a path breaking paper, economist Paulo Maro[5] showed that, highly corrupt nations, have a smaller share of their gross domestic products going into investment. Corruption raises the cost of business and deter would be investors. Fourth, the World Bank Report of 1997 points out that, bribes are not only a disincentive to further investments, because of the immediate costs, but also because they entangle the business in a *"web of time consuming and economically unproductive relations"*. Fifth, corrupt regimes are intrinsically arbitrary and they introduce risks of uncertainty, that many investors are simply, not willing to take. This also automatically raises the transaction cost of investment. As a result, key economic objectives like job creation, development of small and medium enterprises suffer.

In worst case scenarios, the very choice of a project is determined by corruption. Some examples of this kind of corruption are, purchase of technology, which is totally unsuited to the needs of a country or the choice of a capital intensive project, because it is more lucrative in terms of corruption than a labour intensive one, that would have been more beneficial to the development of a country. Thus, real development priorities of a country are thrown to the wind in pursuit of corruption as it helps decision-makers to amass large fortunes. It may be mentioned in this connection, that Africa is littered with deserted motorways, which are now being eroded by savannahs or empty factories, that had fallen into ruin only a few years after they were opened. These *"follies of development"* can be found in many other developing countries and not just in Africa alone[6].

In his work "*Grand Corruption in Third World Development*", George Moody-Sturt, identified areas, which are most vulnerable to corruption. These are most notably the procurement of military and other technically sophisticated equipments and large-scale works. In other words major capital intensive projects and any scheme, where objective evaluation and comparison is hampered, because of the technical sophistication involved. Thus, a country, which borrows money to finance projects which do not satisfy its real needs or which are economically futile and absurd, will witness an exponential rise in its debt burden.

When bribes mean more than votes, a government fails its citizens. The money that could provide public services, is diverted to private bank accounts. The Parliamentary Committee in Philippines calculated that, in 2002 corruption cost the government 1.9 billion annually – twice the size of the national education budget[7]. According to an All India Corruption Study 2005, done by Transparency International, common citizens of the country paid bribes amounting to totally 21,068 crores annually, while availing important public services. This was the largest corruption study, ever undertaken in the country with a sample of 14,405 respondents spread across 20 states.

All this does not mean, that development takes place only when corrupt practices are identified and eliminated and it slows down as corruption spreads. There are examples to show that development and corruption can co-exist for a period of time, but such growth is not sustainable in the long run. Corruption like ignorance, is an enemy of sustainable and equitable development.

International Castigation

Corruption exposes the participants to the risk of international castigation. Issues of corruption now figure prominently in international agenda. It is no longer a taboo subject. After the Lockheed Aircraft scandal in Japan and

Northrop bribery scandal the US, Congress enacted Foreign Corrupt Practices Act in 1977. The Act criminalizes commercial payoffs by American nationals, to public servants abroad. Companies found guilty have to pay heavy fines. Ever since US companies have complained that, they have been forced to compete, on an uneven playing field with their European competitors. But, OECD also followed suit. In December 1997, the convention on Combating Bribery of Foreign Public Officials in International Business Transactions was signed. INTERPOL has now a special working group on corruption. International financial and development institutions have now also woken up, to the negative impact of corruption. The World Bank, which was criticized earlier, for financially dubious and economically risky projects in developing countries, has focused on anti-corruption strategies and measures. It is conducting spot audits of its projects, to catch flagrant misuses of funds.

Reasons for corruption in developing countries

Corruption is widespread in developing and transitional countries, not because the people there are different from elsewhere, but because of prevalence of conditions that facilitate it. In many developing countries watchdog institutions responsible for detection and enforcement are weak. Without powerful anti-corruption mechanisms and presence of able and expert investigators, detection of bribery cases is difficult. Even when there is detection, deterrent punishment is seldom there. This happens more so when corruption is systemic. It is difficult to punish one person severely, when many others are equally guilty. Further, the danger of losing job has a limited deterrent effect, when the official pay is very low.

Studies by the World Bank in the World Development Report, 1997 provides evidence that countries with poorly paid public officials, are more susceptible to corruption. The World Bank has also noted further that "*in general the more favourable the total public sector compensation package compares to compensation to private sector the better is the quality of bureaucracy".* It explicitly cited the example of Singapore. Not surprisingly Singapore, which is widely perceived to have the region's most competent and upright bureaucracy, pays its bureaucrats the best.

However, there is a flaw in this efficiency wage theory that argues that by raising salaries, employers raise the cost to the employees of losing the job. In order to keep the job, the employee will work harder and better. But the efficiency wage theory is premised on the idea, that shirking employees will lose their jobs. In systemically corrupt governments however, employees do not run the risk of losing the job. On the other hands, they may risk their jobs by refusing to participate in ongoing corrupt schemes.

Klitgaard's Equation

Causes of corruption are usually complex and rooted in the country's policy, bureaucratic tradition, political development and social history. Robert Klitgaard[8], devised a formula that lies at the heart of corruption problem. He has used this equation: **C=M+D-A** (C = Corruption, M = Monopoly, D = Discretion, A = Accountability). Corruption takes place when a person has monopoly over the goods and services and has a discretion to decide, who will receive and how much, but is not accountable. Therefore, to reduce for potentials for corruption, it will be necessary to eliminate control of monopoly power, reduce discretion by promoting transparency and also increase accountability standards and practices. Secretiveness has helped politicians and bureaucrats, to keep corrupt practices under wraps. Careful analysis, presentation and dissemination of data, can be effective in raising general awareness, creating momentum for reforms and working out strategies for dealing with corruption. Rose Ackerman[9] has suggested that, competitive services might be an answer to deal with the problem of corruption. If service providers competed, they would beat down the equilibrium level of corruption.

A high level of corruption is exceedingly difficult to reverse. Theoretical models characterize it as sticky. This happens because, increase in corruption creates vested interests, not willing to surrender lightly. Members of the network of corruption, defend their interests by weakening the institutions of restraint and thereby further increasing the level of corruption.

There are fatalists, who feel that chances of success in anti-corruption drive, are limited. It is also time-consuming. They point out that, it took more than a century in England to bring corruption under control. However, there are examples of countries like Hongkong, Singapore, which within a reasonably short time have been able to break out of the corruption trap. Even countries like Botswana, Chili and Malaysia, have attained considerable success in combating corruption. But for effectively tackling corruption, broader social and institutional reforms are necessary. Corruption is very often a symptom of political, economic and institutional malaise. For addressing corruption effectively, these underlying causes have to be tackled. The entrenched nature of corruption requires, some kind of boldness in implementation. Incrementalism is not likely to work. Anti-corruption revolution, if it is to be credible, must start at the top. To make an impact on the public mind, it is necessary to prosecute and punish some major corrupt figures. Some pave-the-path actions are necessary to jolt the system out of the corruption trap.

References

1. Kautilya's Arthasastra, translated by R.Shamasastry (7th ed.: Mysore: Mysore Printing and Publishing House 1961), p. 70.
2. Huntington Samuel P.: Order Interchanging Societies.
3. Daniel Kaufmannand Shan-Jin Wei,1998, "Does 'Grease Money' Speed Up the Wheels of Commerce?" paper presented at the annual meeting of the American Economic Association (Chicago, January).

4. Monograph no. 40. Corruption and Development: Some Perspectives. September 1999.
5. Paulo Maro – Corruption and Growth – Quarterly journal of Economic Vol. 110 (1995) pp 681.713.
6. Effect of Corruption on Development: Dieter Frisch: An Article from The Courier ACP-EU No. 158, July-August 1996: pages 68-70
7. Philippine Daily Inquirer, 6 March 2002, cited in Transparency International
8. Klitgaard, R. 1988. *Controlling Corruption*, Berkeley CA: University of California Press
9. Rose-Ackerman, Susan. 1999. *Corruption and Government: Causes, Consequences, and Reform*. Cambridge: Cambridge University Press

31

Corruption at the Top of the Ladder

The CBI recently conducted simultaneous raids on the premises of A P Singh, a former Chief Secretary of UP and reportedly unearthed ill gotten wealth of more than 100 crore of rupees. The CBI also claimed that this former bureaucrat owned more than 42 properties spread across three states in the names of various family members. In this connection, it may be recalled that the IAS Association of Uttar Pradesh, had earlier in a secret ballot (1996) named him as the *"most corrupt civil servant of the state"* but that did not affect the career prospects of A P Singh. When a delegation of IAS officers met the then Chief Minister of UP, Kalyan Singh and said that there was a case for probing into the acquisition of assets of A P Singh, Kalyan Singh straightway refused to hold such a probe. Under successive Chief Ministers, AP Singh held important posts and his career progression was uninterrupted. Mulayam Singh made him the Chief Secretary of the state and even went to grant him an extension. The case of A P Singh typifies some characteristic features of political and bureaucratic corruption in India, that make it far more sinister and damaging than corruption in other parts of the world.

1. Corruption, in India, occurs upstream and not downstream. This corruption at the top, distorts fundamental decisions about policies, projects and developments.
2. Corruption in India has wings and not wheels. Very often, corrupt gains are smuggled to safe havens abroad and not ploughed back to domestic production and investments.
3. As typically illustrated by this case, corruption often leads to promotion and not prison. In advanced industrial countries as well as in some countries of South-East Asia, notably Japan and South Korea, even the top leaders are not spared. The former Italian Prime Minister Bettino Craxy had to live in exile in Tunisia to escape his extradition due to corruption charges at home.

Unfortunately, in India, corrupt persons are too powerful and beyond accountability. Government departments have built up institutional mechanisms that perpetuate and does not eliminate corruption. Upright officers are frequently transferred to unimportant posts or marginalized, so that corruption chain is not delinked.

One of the main reasons, why corruption has become so endemic and pervasive, especially, among the public servants is because, it has become a high reward and low-risk activity. Very few public servants ultimately get punished. Some kind of a *"law of jungle"*, as a sociologist puts it, prevails. Over 4,000 cases under the Prevention of Corruption Act are pending in different courts of the country. Sometimes junior officers or clerks are punished but senior officers are seldom brought to book. I have never seen in my long service career, that any IAS or IPS officer has been charged, tried, convicted and served a jail sentence under various provisions of the Prevention of Corruption Act. It is reported that since 1990 the Central Vigilance Commission granted sanction for prosecution against

100 civil servants, and so far only one has been convicted by the court of law. Besides criminal cases, departmental proceedings against senior bureaucrats drag on interminably and end in either acquittal or in minor punishment. This happens because, procedure for disciplinary proceedings has become long-drawn out and time consuming. While disciplinary proceedings applicable to the civil servants, observes Santanam Committee in its report "are not dissimilar to those in several other countries, the proceedings for implementing dismissal, removal or reduction in ranks are far more elaborate and formal". There is considerable weight in the recommendation of Santanam Committee that "it should not be unreasonable classification to treat in a separate category charges of bribery, corruption and lack of integrity and provide for simplified procedure."

Unfortunately, bureaucratic corruption prevails because of political corruption. The unholy nexus between corrupt politicians and venal civil servants is well known. This growing nexus between politicians and civil servants, becomes apparent from the Central Vigilance Commission Bill, 2003, passed by the Parliament. It sets up a three member vigilance commission, but makes the employees of central government at the level of joint secretary and above, immune from any enquiry for any offence allegedly committed by them except with the prior approval of the central government. The only rationale given by the government for this differentiation is that, it is essential to protect officers at the decision-making levels and relieve them of their anxiety and likelihood of harassment. Thus, in the newly enacted law, there are two groups of government servants, one comprising those below the level of joint secretary and others of and above, who are to be treated by different yardsticks on the basis that officers at the decision-making levels must be protected. The Central Vigilance Commission Bill is indeed an unconcealed attempt to derail the judgement of Supreme Court in the Vineet Narain's case, which had earlier declared null and void the direction of the Central government known as the "*single directive.*"

The problem of political corruption, which engenders bureaucratic corruption, has been further compounded by the entry of criminals in politics. Many powerful criminals, instead of playing the role of king makers behind the scene, are jumping into the arena of politics and trying to become political leaders themselves. They have both muscle power and money power. There were about 40 tainted Members of Parliament in the 13th Lok Sabha and in the present 14th Lok Sabha, there are about 121 such tainted Members. The National Commission to Review the Working of the Constitution recommended that the Representation of the People's Act, 1951, (RPA) should be amended to provide that any person charged with any offence, punishable with imprisonment, which may extend up to 5 years or more, should be disqualified from contesting the election. If a political party puts up such a candidate with knowledge of his antecedents, it should be de-recognised and de-registered. The National Commission further recommended that the criminal cases against politicians pending for trial or in appeal must be disposed of by appointing special courts. However, our political masters are in no mood to pay any heed to these recommendations.

The situation is further compounded by the fact that the instruments for fighting corruption are getting blunted. The charter for premier investigating agency of the country, namely the Central Bureau of Investigation (CBI), has been widened to deal with various other forms of crimes not connected with corruption. It is now saddled with all kinds of cases by the government and also the Courts. With a strength of 600-700 officers spread all over the country, CBI is not in a position to investigate and prosecute more than 1000 cases in a year. This hardly makes any dent, especially when such cases come up for trial after several years.

Anti-corruption wings in different states have also become politicized and fail to play any useful role in preventing corruption. The heads of anti-corruption wings of different states, are used to further partisan ends by the ruling party. The vigilance chief is not permitted to submit charge sheet against senior government servants, without the clearance of the government. If the arraigned government servant is close to the powers-that-be, the permission is invariably withheld. Recently the Central Vigilance Commission has made public "*black list*" of officers, against whom sanction for prosecution has been needlessly delayed. In the majority of the cases, the CBI has sent repeated reminders to Ministry and the Departments concerned to give the sanction but without any success. The Customs Department alone, as reported in the press, is holding up sanction in 12 cases involving 55 officers, who had been booked by the CBI in the year 2003.

In the case of Vineet Narayan, known popularly as the "Hawala" case, the Supreme Court laid down some proceedings, to insulate the CBI and the Enforcement Directorate from extraneous pressures. There is a similar need to identify other sensitive posts in the government, which can be filled up from a panel of names recommended by an objective and independent Committee. The composition of the committee can be different for different posts. Once selected, the incumbent should have a minimum tenure of two to three years. This may bring about a change in the present situation in which the corrupt elements literally bribe their way to important posts. In a recent forthright interview, the present Director of CBI has clearly admitted that the autonomy of the agency is a *"myth"* and there are constant pulls and pressures to go soft on sensitive areas. Nevertheless, the fixed term will give some elbowroom to the upright officers to withstand pressures. Further, Prevention of Corruption Act, 1986, should be revised to make it more effective. There should be provision to attach properties of government servants, who are facing trials for acts of serious corruption and in possession of disproportionate assets.

The hard fact however remains that the foremost requirement in the battle against corruption is a strong political will and no anti-corruption agenda will be successful, if this is missing. Here lies the rub. The political will is sadly missing. The Bill to set up the institution of Lok Pal is gathering dust because of lack of political consensus. A powerful independent and effective institutional mechanism can play a significant role in curbing corruption. The Independent Commission Against Corruption (ICAC) setup in 1974 in Hong Kong, has done a remarkable job in reducing corruption and enabling Hong Kong to break out of the corruption trap. The then Governor, Sir Murray Maclehose, made it independent of any department and responsible to him only. From its inception, ICAC has adopted a policy that anti-corruption work requires more than just investigation and prosecution. It has a branch, concerned with prevention, which seeks to reduce opportunity for corruption and another, whose task is to involve the public. The government indicated its commitment by appointing a person of unimpeachable integrity to head the ICAC and also by prosecuting some big fish. Singapore has also devised similar institutions and made a successful transition from high corruption to low corruption economy.

Another disquieting factor is that corruption has become legitimised in Indian society, particularly, among the Indian middle class, which provides the overwhelming majority of the public servants. It no longer provokes a sense of outrage or moral indignation. A corrupt public servant, particularly, if he is rich and powerful is no longer held in disrespect or ostracized. This deadening of social conscience and lack of disapproval has provided further stimulant for corruption and aggrandizement by public servants.

32

Telgi Scam and Exposure of Police Corruption

The multi-crore Telgi scam has irretrievably besmirched the reputation and fair name of Mumbai police. The fact that senior officers of Mumbai police, including its Commissioner, are involved in this scam is shocking. The press reports indicate that investigation of the scam will further expose the involvement of a number of other bureaucrats and politicians.

So long the Mumbai police enjoyed good reputation for its professional efficiency. It commanded confidence of the public. It has been led by some stalwarts of the Indian police, like Kanetkar, Julio Riebeiro, Inamdar and many others, who were professionally competent and bolt upright. It has a number middle-ranking officers, enjoying good reputation for their integrity and commitment. However, constant political interference and misuse of the police for partisan political ends over the years, have taken its toll. The situation worsened, when the present Home Minister of Maharashtra started brazenly interfering for ulterior ends in the promotion and transfer of officers. The cancer spread fast. The upright and committed officers, who were not willing to toe the line and dance to his tune, were sidelined and harassed. Plum posts went to officers of questionable reputation. Instances of unsavoury goings–on in the Mumbai police and gradual setting in of the rot were known to many associated with the police. And now this scam of gargantuan proportions has brought it to the full glare of publicity.

In India, corruption in police, is not a new phenomenon. Even the Police Commission of 1902, spoke about alarming corruption and malpractices of Police *Darogas.* Poor pay, lack of training and vast powers were some of the causative factors. The Bihar Police Commission (1960) quoted the saying of Sir John Shore "that subordinate police officers in India ,were paid so low as almost to justify corruption". Though corruption has been rampant among the subordinate ranks of the police, yet the senior officers, by and large, for quite some time were not tainted by it.

Even in the early sixties, when I joined service and was posted in Orissa, the number of senior officers of questionable integrity in both IAS and IPS could be counted on fingers. The Inspector General of Police exercised command and control over his officers. Political interference in posting and transfer of officers and meddling in police administration to further partisan political ends were exceptions rather than the rule.

The situation during the last two decades has undergone a sinister transformation. A nexus has developed between the political masters and police officers of different ranks. The head of the police has now very little say in the transfer and posting of officers in sensitive posts. More often than not, these are decided by the political masters on considerations other than merit. Similarly, in districts posting of officers in police stations is no longer a prerogative of the SP. According to one estimate, in 80% out of nearly 12000 police stations of the country, the District Superintendents of Police do not have any choice in the posting of the officers incharge of police stations. This has severely eroded the line of command and control and given fillip to rampant corruption.

It may be mentioned in this connection, that a study made by the Indian Institute of Public Opinion (IIPO) disclosed that of the several factors responsible for sullying the police image in India, corruption among the policemen was given the highest priority by the respondents spread over four cities in different regions of the country. The problem is compounded by the fact that now many senior officers are also indulging in brazen acts of corruption by joining hands with the subordinate officers. This is ominous because corruption has a systemic character to it. Once it gets started, it tends to spread through the organisation, affecting all its parts. Further, it has a pre-emptive quality. It prevents police leaders from exercising effective control over their subordinates and curtail the organization's capacity of dealing with the full range of problems related to improving the quality of the police service. Unfortunately, senior officers of questionable integrity are favoured by many politicians as they prove to be more malleable and amenable to pressures.

The Chief Minister of Maharashtra is now trying to stem the rot and set things right. He has spoken of the need to cleanse the Mumbai police and refurbish its image. However, for achieving this laudable goal, some administrative transfers and patchwork solutions will not work. If he really wants a clean break, he must sincerely try to implement the important structural reforms recommended by the National Police Commission and subsequently endorsed by the National Human Rights Commission. These are:

(a) Insulation of the investigative wing of the police from external pressures and ensuring its freedom in the operational areas of police investigations;

(b) Removal of the proverbial Damocles' Sword of transfer dangling over the head of the chief of the police and assuring him of a statutory tenure after careful selection;

(c) Constitution of State Security Commission to help the state government to discharge its superintending responsibility, under the framework of law. The State Security Commission should function, as a forum of appeal for disposing of representations of police officers, subjected to illegal order in the performance of their duties. It is worth mentioning in this connection, that in Japan, Civilian Police Safety Commission supervise the police work and operations and also take steps to insulate police from extraneous political pressures. It is also worth noting that in some states today, the average tenure of the Superintendents of Police is between two to six months. Transfers are made on most whimsical grounds. In Vineet Narain's case (better known as Hawala case), the Supreme Court also spoke of the need for the state governments to set up credible mechanisms for the selection, transfer and posting of not only the chief of the police but all officers of the rank of Superintendents of Police and above.

Unfortunately, neither the Central nor the State governments are willing to de-politicise the Indian police. The late Home Minister Indrajit Gupta, wrote to all the Chief Ministers emphasizing, the urgency of implementing the structural reforms recommended by the National Police Commission. He held that qualitative improvement in crime control and order maintenance is not possible without meaningful police reforms. There was predictably no response from any of the Chief Ministers. A PIL has been filed with the Supreme Court for directing the Central and State governments to implement the core recommendations of the National Police Commission. The National Human Rights Commission has impleaded itself as a party to it.

Admittedly, police corruption cannot be contained unless institutional mechanisms are set up to insulate it from extraneous pulls and pressures. In America, direct link between partisan politics and police, has been broken in many states and cities through administrative devices. Now it is necessary for the civil society and the press to vigorously advocate for police reforms and mobilise public opinion to force the hands of the politicians. Insulation of the police from political pressure has to be accompanied by selection of upright police chiefs and enforcement of a slew of in-house reforms to curb police malpractices.

33

Corruption Among the Public Servants in India

In a chapter entitled "Ascertaining by temptations purity or impurity in the character of a Minister", Kautilya goes to elaborate the various types of corruption, to which a prospective minister is subjected. Another chapter of Arthashastra called "Detection of what is embezzled by government servants out of state's revenue", reads almost like a modern official report on modes of corruption and corresponding punishment.

British Rule

In India, during the early stages of the British rule, corruption was widespread. Even some of the main architects of the British rule, which started from the middle of 18th Century, Robert Clive and Governor General Warren Hastings had to face impeachment on charges of corruption and maladministration on their return to England. However, the British rulers in later years, were able to establish in India, a higher civil service, which was honest, competent, well paid and manned both by indigenous and colonial personnel. In due course, Indians came to be admitted to the Civil Services. The members of the civil service, both Indian and British, acquired reputation of being honest and efficient. But it was found difficult to enforce rigid standards at lower levels of administration.

Till about the beginning of the Second World War, corruption was prevalent in considerable measure, among police, revenue, excise and public works departments, particularly, at lower grades. The higher ranks were comparatively free from this evil. "Smaller the compass of state activities, the great depression and lack of fluid resources, set limits to the opportunities and the capacity to be corrupt and be corrupted."[2]

With the beginning of the Second World War, a completely different situation developed. The immense war efforts during 1939 to 1945, which involved annual expenditure of hundreds of crores of rupees, over all kinds of war supplies, created opportunities for accumulation of wealth by dubious means. The wartime scarcities and controls, provided ample opportunities of bribery and favouritism. "It would not be far wrong to say", observes Santanam committee "that the high water mark of corruption was reached in India, as perhaps in other countries, during the period of Second World War."

Even after independence, the situation, instead of improving, deteriorated further. A Committee headed by K Santanam (a Member of Parliament), was set up in 1962 by the Government of India to review the existing instruments for combating corruption and suggest practical steps to make them more effective. The Santanam Committee report was a penetrating study of the problem of corruption and maladministration, prevalent during the sixties. At that time, it was considered one of the most ambitious studies in corruption, in South-East Asia. Santanam Committee noted that corruption has further spread and it was no longer confined to the lower ranks of public servants. The number of senior officers involved was disturbingly large.

The Santanam Committee has also referred to the wrong and exaggerated impression of corruption, especially, among the officers at high levels. It states "we heard from all sides, that corruption had in recent years spread, even to those levels of administration from which, it was conspicuously absent in the past.......... The general impressions are unfair and exaggerated but the very fact such impressions are there, caused damage to the social fabric"[3]. In this connection, it may be mentioned that Gunar Myrdal[4] in his book, "Asian Drama" speaks of *"folklore of corruption in Asian countries"* i.e., people's belief about corruption and emotions attached to those beliefs, as disclosed in public debate and gossips. "The folklore has a crucial bearing, on how people conduct their private lives and how they view their government's efforts to consolidate the nation and direct and spur development."

Corruption Perception Index

Transparency International, a Berlin based NGO, brings out the Corruption Perception Index and ranks countries according to the level of corruption assessed by those, who do business with the country. Transparency International's Corruption Perception Index of 2003, indicates the level of corruption in 133 countries. Maximum score is 10, indicating the country is least corrupt, minimum score is 0, indicating, that the country is highly corrupt. India scores 2.8 and is at 83rd rank and is perceived to be one of the most corrupt countries. India's position in this respect is far worse than that of China's 66th, position with a score of 3.4.

The level of corruption among the public servants is staggering. According to Transparency International report of 2002, bribes paid to public servants amounts to $ 6.2 million per year. A survey done by an Indian firm (ORG-MARG), on behalf of Transparency showed that some of the most corrupt sectors in government are education, health, police, power and judiciary, etc. A Confederation of Indian Industries (CII), quotes a study of 160 industries in Bangalore, Mumbai and Ahmedabad. It says that a third of them pay over Rs. 5,000 in slush money every month to the Inspector. The annual cost of small and medium enterprises satisfying the Inspector Raj is as high as Rs. 300 crores. The CII study shows that liberalization in India might have done away with the license raj but the '*inspector raj*' still continues.

Definition of Public Servant

The Prevention of Corruption Act 1988, which replaced the Prevention of Corruption Act, 1947 widened the definition of the Public Servant. Clause VIII of Section 2 of the Act provides that the public servant is "any person who holds an office by virtue of which he is authorized or required to perform public duty". The public duty has now been defined in Section 2(b) of the Act "Public duty means a duty in discharge of which the state, the public or the community at large, has an interest". The Act of 1988 now brings within its sweep, each and every person, who held an office by virtue of which, he is required to perform a public duty. The Supreme Court in the case J. Jayalalitha vs. Union of India[5], observed that "while replacing the 1947 Act by the present Act of 1988, the legislature wanted to make the Act more effective and widen the scope of the Act, by giving a wider definition of the word public servant". The Court further went on to say:

"Corruption corrodes the moral fabric of the society and corruption by public servant not only leads to corrosion of the moral fabric of society but is harmful to national economy and national interest as the persons occupying high posts in government by misusing their power due to corruption can cause considerable damage to national economy, national interest and image of the country."

In India, unfortunately, corruption has spread alarmingly among the senior public servants also. When India became independent, senior officers, by and large, were regarded as efficient and devoted to their responsibility. They were also subjected to fairly rigorous government servant conduct rules.

But unfortunately the decline in the standard of probity of the Indian bureaucracy has been alarming. According to the verdict of a Hong Kong based think tank called *"Political and Economic Risk Consultancy"*, based upon the annual survey of those, who are interacting with the bureaucracy of Asian countries, on a 10-point scale Singapore was rated, as the best at 2.53 and Vietnam worst at 8.9. India with 8 points occupied the 9th position among the 12 Asian countries[6]. This is, indeed, a very depressing state of affairs for a country, once proud of the quality of administration and dedication of its senior officers.

An Indian newspaper Economic Times made the following comments, about this report in its editorial on 11th March, 1998. "This is indeed a sorry state of affairs for a country, which was once proud of the quality of its administration, the dedication of its bureaucratic personnel and the knowledge they employed. On all counts, our collective confidence in our institution of administration is severely eroded. The unacceptable quality of India's administration today is that it increases the transaction cost, inhibits market forces, wastes public money and thrives on an ideology by which, the state takes on unnecessary tasks, while being unable to perform its basic functions."

It is argued by some writers that corruption and bribery are necessary lubricants for a cumbersome system of administration. But this *"grease the wheel"* argument is untenable. *Speed money* belying the name, has the effect of slowing down the pace of administration further. Delay will be deliberately caused, in order to invite payments of bribe. Sometime, even the payment of bribe does not help; because there is a multiple veto power system in operation. A high official in Delhi reportedly told a friend that if you want him to move a file, he is not sure if he can be of help. But if you want him to stop a file, he can do it immediately. This ability to stop a file at multiple points (installed to keep check on corrupt officials), does actually increase corruption as well as inefficiency.

Sometimes, it is also argued that, corruption can have a desirable distributive impact as it shifts income and wealth from the richer individuals and companies to the poorer ones. These arguments advanced in support of corruption at micro level, are indeed fallacious from macro point of view. Corruption, even when it is petty and routine, cannot be a means of stimulating economic growth and improving living standards. It causes illegal transfer of state revenue to richer and private individuals, who are in a position to pay bribes to the detriment of those, who cannot. Indeed, the evil effects of corruption far outweigh the so called benefits. The UNDP report on *Human Development in South Asia 1999 – the Crisis of Governance* says, if corruption levels in India were reduced to those of Scandinavian countries, investment in the country will increase annually by 12% and GDP growth by almost 1.5%[7].

Paolo Mauro[8], in his study on corruption and growth, established the negative relationship between corruption and economic growth for a number of developing countries. It is sometimes difficult to assess the indirect cost of corruption, but frequently, they exceed the direct costs. Sometimes valuable resources are wasted on project to that may provide opportunities for substantial grafts. In consequence, projects favouring social economic sectors such as health, housing and education suffer. Several studies on Asian countries (viz. Indonesia) brought out that their governments, thanks to procurement frauds, paid 20 to 100 percent more for goods and services than they should have[9]. Corruption also hampers entrepreneurship and intellectual pursuits. Many bright persons, instead of following the straight path, try to explore ways and means of getting round the system. They feel that it is not necessary to waste time and effort in developing a business career, when one can enjoy large income from cut money in a suitable government employment.

Robert Klitgaard[10] devised a formula, which lies at the heart of the corruption problem. It equals corruption with monopoly power, plus discretion minus accountability and low government salary. Corruption takes place, when a person has monopoly power over goods and services and a discretion to decide, who will receive it and how much and is not accountable and has a low-income level. The solution to the problem of corruption needs reduction of artificial monopoly power, limited official discretion, enhancement of transparency, punishment for the violators and reducing the direct incentives for engaging in corrupt activities. Monopoly power without discretion or discretion without monopoly power gives limited opportunities for corruption, but the combination can be lethal. The more discretion government officials have over operation of business or people's lives, there remains greater chances of corruption.

Many Outdated Laws

Turning to Indian scene, one sees that there are many laws and rules in existence, which perpetuate corruption and give opportunities for corrupt practices among the government officials. For example, it requires nearly 47 different approvals to construct a building in Mumbai and a small-scale entrepreneur has to handle 36 different inspectors each month and 46 different documents[11]. A committee was appointed by the Government of India (Jain Committee), to identify the administrative laws, which were obsolete. The committee identified 3500 laws, which could be scrapped. In order to promote a corruption free government, there should be a systematic campaign to remove from the statute books the obsolete laws that clutter them. There is need to have the concept of sunset principle, as in the USA, so that the no rules or regulations should be in the statute book forever.

It is often seen that malpractices remain unchecked, because most of the government departments have built up institutional mechanisms that perpetuate and not eliminate corruption. Upright officers, who refuse to be corrupt are frequently transferred to unimportant posts or marginalized so that the corruption chain is not de-linked. In this connection, it may be mentioned that Santanam Committee on Prevention of

Corruption, in its report, recommended to the government that since corruption was closely related to administrative procedures and abuse of discretion, the Central Vigilance Commission (CVC), which they proposed to set up, should deal not only with complaints against corruption but also hear complaints against wrong, dilatory administrative procedures and exercises. The committee wrote to the then Prime Minster, Lal Bahadur Shastri "in order to effectively deal with the problem, it is necessary to take into consideration the root causes, of which the most important is, the wide discretionary power which has to be exercised by the executive, in carrying on the complicated work of modern administration". However, the Government of India, was not in favour of empowering the CVC, with the job of looking into the grievances of the citizens, against unfair administrative practices and procedures. So, it ordered that the CVC should only look into the matters relating to corruption. It promised, that the Department of Administrative Reforms, would work out the details of such an institution. This promise has remained unfulfilled. Thus, the CVC could not play the role of ombudsman as in UK and other western countries.

De-regulation

The oft-repeated assumption that deregulation and privatization can significantly reduce corruption is perhaps not correct. These are not magic wands that can eliminate corruption overnight. Experience in countries like Russia, China, India has shown that deregulation can in fact increase corruption. It is seen very often that corrupt rulers are keen to privatize state assets for large one-time gains. Regulatory committees, set up by the government in the process of deregulation, can be and indeed are corrupted by businessmen and monopolists. It is necessary, therefore, that institutional structures of regulatory agencies are worked out before bidding, in order to prevent manipulation. Often, there is nexus between politicians involved in selling state assets and their cronies buying them.

Political Corruption

However, unsurprisingly the most important factor behind the cancerous growth of corruption in public service has been the unholy nexus that has grown up between the corrupt politicians and venal civil servants. Politicians have their own compulsions. Today, elections have become prohibitively expensive. Election expenditure is 20 to 30 times more than the legal ceiling on expenses prescribed. These expenditures can be sustained only when the return is high. The return can be high only when high levels of corruption are sustained over a long period of time, leading to institutionalization of corruption. In consequence, political masters rely on civil servants, considered malleable and dependable. Honest officers are marginalised and dishonest officers get plum postings.

The nexus between the politicians and civil servants becomes apparent from the Central Vigilance Commission Bill, 2003, passed by the Parliament, which sets up a 3 Member Vigilance Commission. It makes employees of the central government, at the level of the joint secretary and above, immune from any enquiry into any offence allegedly committed by them, except with the prior approval by the Central Government. The only rationale offered by the government for this differentiation is that it is essential to protect officers at decision making levels and to relieve them of the anxiety and likelihood of harassments for making honest decisions. Thus, in the newly enacted law, there are two groups of government servants - one comprising those below the level of joint secretary and others of and above, who are to be treated by different yardsticks, on the basis that officers at decision making levels must be protected. In the Parliamentary forms of democracy, the ultimate decision is taken by the Minister. Only the Minister is answerable to the Parliament and not the secretary, additional secretary or the joint secretary. Therefore, in the matters of so called decision-making "treating equals unequally is discriminatory and violative of equality clause of the constitution[13]".

The Central Vigilance Commission Bill is indeed an attempt to derail the judgement of the Supreme Court in Vineet Narain's case, which had earlier declared null and void, the impugned directions of the central government, known as single directive[13].

The problem of political corruption has been further compounded by the entry of the criminal in politics. According to the report of a committee, appointed by the Government of India (Vohra Committee) "all over India, crime syndicates have become law unto themselves .... Even in small towns and villages, musclemen have become order of the day. The nexus between criminal gangs, police and politicians have come out clearly in various parts of the country. Mafia network is virtually running a parallel government, pushing the state into irrelevance[14]".

Many powerful criminals instead of playing the role of kingmakers behind the scene are jumping into the arena of politics and becoming political leaders themselves. To counter this ominous trend, some important electoral reforms are called for. The National Commission to Review the Working of the Constitution, which was set up by the Government of India to examine as to how best the constitution can respond to the challenges and needs of efficient, smooth, effective system of governance. The Commission has also takes stock of socio-economic development of modern India, within the frame work of parliamentary democracy and recommend the changes, that are required in the provisions of the constitution, without interfering with its basic features.

No Punishment

One of the main reasons, why corruption has become so endemic and pervasive, especially, among the public servants is because it has become a high reward and low risk activity. Very few public servants ultimately get punished. Some kind of a "Law of Jungle prevails", as a sociologist puts it.

Further, departmental proceedings against senior public bureaucrats drag on interminably and end in either acquittal or with minor punishment. This happens because, procedures for disciplinary proceedings have become long-drawn-out. "While disciplinary proceedings applicable to civil servants", observes Santanam Committee in its report, "are not dissimilar to those in several other countries, the proceedings for implementing dismissal, removal, reduction in ranks, are far more elaborate and formal[15]."

This is mainly due to the way, in which the courts have interpreted Article 311 of the Constitution. Article 311(2)(1)(a) of the Constitution provides that "no person, who is a member of civil services of India or an all India service or civil services of a state or holds a civil post under the union or a state, shall be dismissed by an authority subordinate to that by which he was appointed. (b), No such person, as aforesaid shall be dismissed or removed or reduced in rank, except after an enquiry, in which he has been informed of the charges against him and given an opportunity of being heard in respect of those charges."

In a number of cases, the Supreme Court and state High courts have observed, that the word "reasonable" must mean according to the rules of natural justice. But the fact that the rules of natural justice have not been completely and precisely determined has enabled the courts to prescribe various restrictive conditions.

The cardinal principle of departmental enquiry is that, it should be initiated and completed expeditiously. That is why a different procedure, free from the restrictions of the Indian Evidence Act, has been prescribed. But in practice, departmental proceedings have become quite involved and intricate. The civil servants in India, enjoy protection, not available to their counterparts in many other countries. "In USA, when it is proposed to dismiss, remove or demote any federal employee, he cannot claim any trial or hearing. which is granted, at the discretion of the department concerned. Such an employee is required to submit a written reply in his defence, within a short time. In UK, matter of this sort, is dealt with entirely through *'usual channels'* and the final authority in each department is the Minister himself, advised by the Permanent Secretary. Disciplinary proceedings are conducted without undue formality. There is no standard practice, which should be applicable to every case, though care is taken that no government servant is punished, unless he has been given an opportunity to defend himself[16]". There is considerable weight in the recommendation of the Santanam Committee that "it should not be an unreasonable classification to treat in a separate category charges of bribery, corruption and lack of integrity and provide for simplified procedure."

Poor Salaries

The poor salaries paid to public servants are perhaps, another causative factor behind exponential increase in corruption. Studies for the World Bankin World Development Report, 1997, provides evidence that countries with poorly paid public officials are more susceptible to corruption. In India, with rising inflation, there has been a steady erosion of the real income of the public servants. There also prevailed among the policy makers "a mistaken impression, that impoverishment of higher bureaucracy was an essential ingredient of socialist pattern of society[17]."

Now following the recommendations of the Fifth Central Pay Commission. There has been some improvement in the pay scale of government servants, but even then, it is not comparable to what is paid by private sector to its employees. In this connection, it bares mention that the Government of Singapore adopted and implemented some of the principles identified by the World Bank in its report titled *"Policy Research – Asian Miracle, Economic Growth and Public Policy for ensuring probity in Public Service."*

The principles are:

1. Recruitment and promotion must be merit based and highly competitive;
2. Total compensation, including, the perks and prestiges, must be competitive with the private sector and
3. Those who make it to the top must be amply rewarded[18].

The World Bank noted further "in general, the more favourable total public sector compensation package compares to compensation in the private sector, the better is the quality of the bureaucracy". It explicitly cited the example of Singapore. "Not surprisingly, Singapore which is widely perceived to have the region's most competent and upright bureaucracy pays its bureaucrats best."

Though improvement of salaries is expected to lessen corrupt propensities among the public servants, there is also hard evidence of many anti-corruption investigators that corruption is habit forming, once an officer starts taking bribes. This streak can be seen among the senior officers also. It develops into a habit and he cannot resist himself whenever an opportunity for illegal gratification comes. Very often, the modus operandi remain the same.

Blunting of anti-corruption Instruments

Unfortunately, instruments for fighting corruption are getting blunted. The charter for the premier investigation agency of the country, namely Central Bureau of Investigation (CBI), has been widened to deal with various others forms of cases not connected with corruption. With a strength of investigating officers spread all over the country, the CBI could prosecute more than 1000 corruption cases every year. This is now being argumented to handle ever rising arrears of cases in CBI and High/Supreme courts. Such cases are decided after long years of trial. Unfortunately, anti-corruption agencies or vigilance organisations of many states, have become politicized, and often used for political witch-hunt rather than preventing corruption.

In some states it has become a practice to launch criminal cases against political opponents, when a new party comes to power. Unfortunately, very few cases are thoroughly investigated and resolutely pursued in the courts of law. As a result, political leaders charged with corruption are seldom brought to book. They only stand tarnished in the eyes of the public and develop a highly cynical attitude towards corruption. The head of anti-corruption agencies of different states often act as the hatchet men of the government. The vigilance chief is not permitted to present charge sheet without clearance of the government, and if the arraigned government servant is close to the powers-that-be, the permission is withheld. While, over-all control of the government over anti-corruption wings is understandable, control over the registration of cases and submission of final forms is contrary to the provisions of the criminal procedure code.

International Double Standards

There is also international double standard in dealing with corruption. Many international donors try to restrict and curtail loans and aids to developing countries, without taking note of the international dimension of corruption where it is rampant. Some of the western countries, with the commendable exception of the United States of America, regard commissions and bribes paid by the multinationals as legitimate expenses of business. These expenses are also tax deductible[19]. There is need for developed countries to change current laws and practices and declare all bribes paid by the firms as punishable offences. They should declare bribery illegal, whether it is paid to foreign officials or national residents.

Strategies to Combat Corruption

The Law Commission in India, in its *167th* Report suggested enactment of Corrupt Public Servants (Forfeiture of Property) Act. The Bill for enacting this act has been *pending since February, 1994*. The main provisions of this Act include: (a) it shall not be lawful for any person to hold illegally acquired property either by himself or through any person for his benefit (b) where any person holds any illegally acquired property, such property shall be liable for forfeiture by the government (c) any person holding any illegally acquired property on conviction by a criminal court, should also be liable to punishment of imprisonment, which shall not be less than 7 years and which can extend to 14 years.

In addition to passing fresh legislation like Corrupt Public Servants (Forfeiture of Property) Act, it is necessary to ensure that the existing laws, which relate to checking of corruption, are effectively implemented. For example, the Benami Transaction Prohibition Act, 1998, enabling confiscation of Benami property, has so far remained a dead letter. Under Section 8 of this Act, the Government has to prescribe rules, under which confiscation can take place. The rules have not been framed so far explicably. The National Commission to Review the Constitution has recommended that the union government, without any further loss of time, should frame rules under Section 8 of the Act for acquiring Benami property.

It is often seen that the political bosses are able to pressurize the bureaucrats to fall in line, through the instrumentality of transfers and postings. In the case of Vineet Narayan[20], popularly known as the Hawala Case, the Supreme Court laid down procedures to insulate CBI and Enforcement Directorate from extraneous pressures. It is also necessary to identify other sensitive positions in government, which can be filled up from a panel of names, recommended by an objective and independent committee. Composition of the committee can be different for different posts. Once selected, the incumbent should have a minimum tenure of two to three years. This will being about a change in the present situation in which, the corrupt elements literally bribe their way into important posts.

Whistleblower Act

There is need to have a whistleblowers act to provide immunity to the informers. Many western countries have

Whistleblowers Act to prevent employers from taking retributive action against the whistle-blowers. The term blow the whistle is a relatively recent entry into the vocabulary of public and corporate affairs incarnated by whistle-blowers. It means, the process by which insiders go public with claims of malpractices by or within organisations, after failing to remedy the matter from inside and often at great risk to themselves. It is this willingness to stand up for a principle and court risks openly, that distinguishes whistle-blowing from related practices like in-house criticism, anonymous leaks and the like. Several western countries have enacted Public Interest Disclosure Act to fight corruption and mal administration. The United States Whistle Blower Protect Act, 1989 (amended in 1994), protects public interest disclosures by federal employees. In the United Kingdom, Public Interest Disclosure Act, 1998, provides protection to employees working in the public, private and non-profit sectors, including those working outside the United Kingdom. South Africa also has followed the UK example, through its Protected Disclosure Act of 2000. In India, there is an urgent need for such an act to protect informants against retribution or any form of discrimination for reporting, what they perceive to be wrong, which during enquiry may ultimately turn out to be not entirely or substantially true. There was recently a tragic case of one whistle-blower, named Satyandra Dubey of Bihar, who was done to death by the mafia for exposing malpractices in the construction of National Highways. The Government of India's Resolution of April 2004, empowers the Central Vigilance Commission to act on the complaints of whistle-blowers and protect them. It is hoped that an effective Whistleblowers' Act will follow.

Right to Information

An effective Right to Information Act will strengthen the hands of the citizens to combat corruption. New law RTI Act, 2005, has been enacted. It is essential that the government policies and programs become transparent and people are able to exercise their right to information. The public had only limited facilities to get details of administrative and financial transactions of the government agencies. On the other hand, in developed countries, people have the right to access to papers of the government, except those pertaining to security. People's right to information, will make the working of the government more transparent and will be an effective antidote to corruption[21]. The experience of using IT (Information Technology) in passenger reservation system in Railways or the Registration offices in Andhra Pradesh shows how information technology can be an important instrument for better and cleaner governance. People's right to information will make the working of government more transparent and will act as effective antidote to corruption. Sunlight is always the best disinfectant.

A proactive judiciary is also the need of the hour. There is a prevailing impression that accused persons in corruption cases are not severely punished by the courts. The courts often take an indulgent attitude. Corruption in judiciary is another problem, which is very often not discussed because of the Contempt of Court Act. The National Commission to Review the Working of the Constitution has suggested appropriate constitutional amendments enabling citizens to use "right of freedom of speech" for presenting the truth without fear of contempt.

Property Returns

Public officials must submit every year, a detailed breakdown of assets positions and tax returns. If the property returns are carefully scrutinized and followed by swift inquiries against some of the known corrupt public servants, it will have a salutary deterrent effect. Existing provision in Government Servants Conduct Rules regarding submission of annual property returns is now honoured in breach.

Prevention of Corruption Act, 1988, should be revised to make it more effective. There should be provision to attach the properties of corrupt public servants, who have been trapped while accepting bribes and who are facing trials for possessing disproportionate assets. Presumption of guilt should be made comprehensive to cover all cases of corruption.

There is also need for setting up of powerful and effective institutional mechanisms to curb corruption. In Hong Kong, the Independent Commission Against Corruption (ICAC), has done remarkable job in reducing corruption. The ICAC, set up in 1974 was given the power to investigate and prosecute cases of corruption and also to engage in campaigns of public education. The government indicated its commitment, by appointing a person of unimpeachable integrity to head the ICAC and also by prosecuting some big fish. The commission targets both public and private, as well as petty and high level corruption. It also constantly enlists the support of the public. Singapore has also devised similar institutions and made a successful transition from high corruption to low corruption economy[22].

In India, unfortunately the Bill to set up the institution of Lok Pal (National Ombudsman) is gathering dust. Lok Pal Bill should be enacted into a law as soon as possible and all political functionaries, including the Prime Minister are to be brought under the purview of Lok Pal. It is regrettable that because of lack of political consensus, the matter is getting postponed indefinitely. Indeed, the foremost requirement in the battle against corruption is a strong political will. No anti-corruption agenda will be successful if this is missing. Article 116 of Finland's Constitution makes a Minister liable to prosecution, if he or she has "through gross negligence essentially contravened his/her duties as minister". There is a need to impose precisely similar liability on the country's central as well as state ministers.

Many countries today are witnessing a backlash against corruption. A shift in public tolerance for corruption is taking place and the demand for settling up of institutions for ensuring accountability and transparency of government activities is gathering momentum. In the words of Elliot. "It is a revolution which even Marx could have scarcely predicted. Simultaneous, though largely painful public revolt, against the world's oldest part-time profession, proffering and accepting bribes[23]"

There is now an overriding necessity to involve respected and public-spirited citizens to create social awareness of the corruption menace. The enlightened people and civil society institutions have to play an active role in this cleansing process. Mere reliance on government and its agencies will not help. Unfortunately, a corrupt public leader or public servant, if he is rich and powerful, is no longer held in disrespect or ostracized. This deadening of social conscience has further helped escalation and proliferation of corruption.

References

1. Kautilya's, *Arthasastra*, translated by R. Shamasastry, (7th ed.: Mysore: Mysore Printing and Publishing House 1961) Page 70.
2. *Report of the Santanam Committee*. Government of India Publication on Corruption, 1964 Page 6.
3. Ibid, Page 11.
4. *Asian Drama - An enquiry into the poverty of nations*. An abridgement by Seth. S. King of the Twentieth Century Fund Study, Page 202.
5. AIR I, 1999 Supreme Court 1912, Page 1922.
6. *Assessment of Asian Bureaucracies* by Political and Economic Risk Consultancy. Hong Kong 1998.
7. Human Development in South Asia 1999 – the Crisis of Governance. Oxford Chapter 5, *The Corruption Menace,* Page 98.
8. Paolo Mauro. *Corruption and Growth.* Quarterly Journal of Economic, August 1995. Why worry about corruption?
9. Asian Development Bank. *Anti-Corruption Policies* June, 1998.

10. Klitgaard, R, 1988. *Controlling Corruption*. Berkley: University of California press.
11. Gandhi R. 1997, *Combating Corruption: a National Agenda,* Report prepared by Indian Merchant's Chambers and McKinsey's 21 December 1997, Mumbai.
12. Fasli Nariman. *Senior officers must not be spared. There is fatal flaw in the CVC bill.* Published in Tribune August 12, 2003.
13. *Vineet Narain vs Union of India*, AIR 1998 SC 889.
14. *Report of the National Commission to Review the working of the Constitution*, Chapter 4, Page 8.
15. *Report of the Santanam Committee*, Page 34.
16. Ibid, paragraph 5.7, Page 34.
17. *Report of the Fifth Pay Commission*, Vol 3, Government of India, publication. Page 1574.
18. Policy Research – *The Asian Miracle, Economic Growth and Public Policy*, World Bank, Oxford University Press, 1993, Page 175-176.
19. *Human Development in South Asia*, op cit Page 8.
20. *Vineet Narain case*; op cit.
21. Gandhi R op cit.
22. UNDP, 1997. *Corruption and Good Governance*. UNDP discussion. Paper No 3.
23. Kimberley and Elliot. *Corruption and Global Economy*. Institute For International Economics. Washington D C June 1997.

34

Combating Terror

Serial bomb blasts by the terrorists at Jaipur, killing nearly 50 people and injuring about 170, have clearly demonstrated their capacity to strike at will with devastating effect at any place of their choosing. The police and security agencies, by and large, remain clueless. Earlier, terrorist bomb blasts at Mumbai, Hyderabad and Varanasi, have remained undetected. The unpredictability of terrorist attacks has heightened public fear and given rise to the apprehension that more such strikes are in the offing. This unpredictability of the danger, which is a psychologically damaging factor, is very much amenable to manipulation by the terrorists.

There is also a shrill and loud cry of intelligence failure. Many political leaders as well as members of the press have castigated the intelligence agencies and also the National Security Advisor for failure to provide precise and timely intelligence about the strike plans of the terrorists. The criticisms, though understandable, are not very fair and correct.

Collection of intelligence about terrorist outfits is an extremely difficult and challenging job that requires careful planning and long-term preparations. Modern terrorists operate through small centrifugal groups. Penetration into one may not throw light on the activities of other groups. Terrorist cells consist of small groups of trained men, who remain unaware of the operations of other cells and hence detection of some operatives does not help in unearthing operations planned by other outfits. Different modus operandi of the terrorist groups, random nature of attacks and the absence of discernible Standard Operating Procedures (SOPs), make it difficult to get reliable advance warning about terrorist attacks. Normally, there are very few Early Warning Indicators (EWIs).

The Intelligence Bureau (IB) is a professional organizations, manned by selected by officers of central intelligence agencies, have been able to foil a number of planned attacks of the terrorists. Their achievements remain unknown and untrumpeted. But operations of many new terrorist cells crouching for the spring remain undetected.

The security scenario, however, remains very grim. According to intelligence estimates, there are a number of organizations working on Indian soil breeding a sense of alienation among the Muslim youth groups and sucking them in the global whirl of Jihad. The collusion of some of the local Muslims with the Jihadis enlarges the scope and magnitude of the terrorist threats in the country. Thus, Jihadi terrorism has now been Indianized and they have been able to set up a number of sleeper cells, swhich can be activated at appropriate time and places. Surprise is the corner stone of any successful terrorist operation. Security forces are always stronger than the terrorists and hence the latter seek to minimize the disadvantage by choosing time, method and location of attacks.

After the blasts, usual blame game has started. BJP leader LK Advani has blamed the UPA government for going soft on terror and failing to enact a strong anti-terror law. The UPA government after coming to power had scrapped POTA because of its reported abuse and misuse against the minorities by the law enforcement authorities. However, the need for strong anti-terror law to combat terrorist menace, cannot be gainsaid. To deal with this omnibus menace, the police need powerful anti-terrorist laws to intercept communications, cutting of supplies of fund, tracing the hideouts and seizing the properties, of the terrorists. After 9/11, the United Nations has also asked member states to pass stringent laws to deal with terrorism and countries like USA, UK have done so. Indeed the country needs special law to combat the hydra-headed monster of terrorism. Some of the States, like Maharashtra, have passed the anti-terrorist law, viz. Maharashtra Control of Organized Crime Act, 1999, which are of great help to the authorities in containing the activities of the terrorists. The act also contains adequate safeguards to prevent its misuse.

I still recollect that the officials of the Home Department of the Government of United Kingdom, who visited the National Human Rights Commission in 1995 (immediately after the non-renewal of TADA by the Parliament) during discussions with us clearly expressed the view that the police and the security forces would not be able to checkmate the terrorists without stringent anti-terrorist laws.

But strong anti-terrorist laws are of little avail unless there are effective and competent agencies to painstakingly investigate the cases and bring the offenders to book. The contours, patterns and modus operandi of the terrorists have now undergone significant changes. Investigation of terrorist crimes, which are often transnational in their ramifications, require specialized expertise of a very high order and States, because of their limited means, find it difficult to provide specialized investigators in large numbers. Indeed, there is a felt need to have a specialized agency for investigation of crimes which are to be viewed as federal crimes. The Malimath Committee in its report on "Reforms of Criminal Justice System" strongly urged in favour of a federal law and a federal investigation agency, which will have an all India character and which will investigate crimes that affect "national security and activity aimed at destabilizing the country". In USA, the FBI is entrusted with the responsibility to investigate and prosecute offences that affect the security of the country. The list of federal crimes in USA includes, offences like terrorism, money laundering, drug trafficking, trading with the enemy, etc. During the last few years, there has been a steady increase in the number of offences declared as federal crimes.

At present, the CBI investigates crimes with interstate linkages with the concurrence of the state governments. A suitable amendment of the constitution would facilitate the enactment of a central legislation. This is necessary because police and public order are state subjects. Perhaps, even without an amendment, it may be possible to classify some offences as federal crimes and entrust the investigation to a central agency, as has been done in the case of NDPS Act and Prevention of Money Laundering Act. But for successful investigation of terrorist crime closest cooperation coordination of the State is necessary. Without this, a central agency will not be able to function effectively.

Besides, strong anti-terrorist law and an efficient federal agency for investigating terrorist crimes, some other measures are also urgently necessary to deal with the darkening situation. First, special branches of state police forces have to be activised by induction of competent officers. At present, most of the state special branches are packed with people, who lack professional expertise and were picked up for considerations other than competence. They are often used for political surveillance, collection of intelligence regarding intra-party and inter-party problems, and not for countering terrorist work and operations. Second, it is necessary to make the public aware of the magnitude and dimensions of terrorist threats and steps necessary to counteract it. Collection of intelligence becomes easy, when police enjoy some degree of public cooperation and confidence in the society. To get reliable information about the Jihadi terrorists groups, police must also enjoy some measure of confidence of the minority groups. The, sensitivities of minority communities cannot be ignored. Third, training, equipping, empowering and motivating officers at cutting edge levels is a must. Fight against terrorism is essentially a foot soldier's battle and not a general's one. Unfortunately, not much has been done to improve the skills, knowledge and operational proficiency of the police officers of different states on the ground.

Fourth, India should draw lessons from the working of the Homeland Security in USA. Since 9/11, not a single terrorist attack has taken place there. The Department of Homeland Security with a variety of alert measures and drills have rebuffed attempts by Al-Qaida and its sympathizers to launch terrorist strikes. Some of the measures, with necessary modifications, keeping in mind our requirements can be introduced.

35

War on Mumbai – India's 9/11

Brutal and devastating terrorist attacks on different places in Mumbai on the night of 26th November, are by far the most vicious and organized acts of terrorist violence the country has so far witnessed. It was an audacious, well planned plot, carried out with ruthless skill and ferocity. The terrorists carefully selected their targets, posh hotels and other landmarks of the city, in order to send a chilling message to the world that India is indeed a soft state where they can strike at their own will.

The attacks were directed against the citizens of USA, UK, Israel and India – crusaders, Zionists and Hindus, and bear clear fingerprints of Al Qaida and their Pakistan based terrorist outfits, Lashkar-I-Toyiba. According to figures released by the government, 172 persons, including, 27 foreigners were killed in the attacks and so many others were injured. But the number might further increase as more bodies may be recovered from the debris of Taj hotel, symbol of Jameshedji Tata's vision of modern India. It was indeed, an audacious terrorist attack of unprecedented magnitude, meticulously planned and carried out with lethal precision. The terrorists knew the nook and cranny of Taj and Oberoi hotels and the Nariman house, where a number of Jews are residing.

Evidence available so far shows that the terrorists came and stayed in the hotels, reconnoitered the places thoroughly and worked out the details of their macabre operational plans. They were trained, brainwashed, equipped with deadly weapons and then despatched for their operations. The object was to devastate India's commercial capital and scare the foreign investors out of the country.

There is, as usual, loud cry about monumental intelligence failure. The fact of the matter is that getting hard intelligence about organization, motivations and operational details of terrorist groups functioning in small and decentralized cells is difficult. But even then, we should have some clues about the unprecedented scale of terrorist violence planned and organized from outside. We are grappling with Jihadi terrorism in J and K for more than two decades but have not been able, unfortunately, to build up good sources in place so far and this seriously limits our capacity to fight against terrorism. The battle against terrorism cannot be won without galvanizing our intelligence apparatus and improving the flow and quality of intelligence. Indeed, in the battle against terrorism, intelligence is the king. Unfortunately, police intelligence set-ups in the States are in a very bad shape. They are now packed with people, who lack professional expertise and have been picked up for considerations other than merit. They are mainly used for political surveillance and collection of intelligence regarding inter party and inner party problems. No wonder, collection of terrorist intelligence is very poor and counter terrorist operations suffer. Even when some nuggets of intelligence are available, these are not properly analyzed and followed up. It seems, some intelligence, regarding terrorists coming to Mumbai by sea and launching attacks on hotels were available, but they were not properly assessed and follow up action was not taken. This happened due to lack of coordination, a malaise that bedevils our intelligence set-up. It is difficult to get pinpointed and predictive intelligence about terrorist operations, but constant preparedness and vigilance can foil many of their attacks.

There is also appalling failure of political leadership to evolve a firm and consistent policy of fighting against terror. It was a grave mistake of UPA government to scrap POTA and adopt a soft and supine policy of combating terror. Misuse of laws is no justification for scrapping it. The answer is to provide mechanisms to prevent their misuse. United Nations has mandated that all states must adopt necessary legal instruments to combat terrorism. Already stringent anti-terrorist laws have been passed by most of the European countries that have not suffered even a fraction of the casualties that have occurred in India. Law enforcement officers, and even a majority of informed members of public, want realistic, stringent anti-terrorist laws that provide more period for police remand, more time for filing charge sheets, make bail provisions far more stringent and confessions before a police officer admissible. The present law to deal with the terrorism, Unlawful Activities Prevention Act (UAPA) does not contain POTA provisions like recording of confessional statement by police officers, interception of wire and electronic communication, etc. A stringent law with draconian provisions to counteract the hydra-headed monster of terrorism is the need of the hour the Malimath Committee recommended Maharashtra Control of Organized Crime Act (MCOCA) as a model anti-terrorist legislation that can be followed by the center and other states. There was also no justification not to give Presidential assent on wooly considerations to anti terrorist logislations passed by Gujarat and Rajasthan State Assemblies. There is crying need for setting up of a Federal Investigating Agency to investigate speedily terrorist crimes which are complex and transnational in character. Now at last, the government has woken up from slumber and thinking in terms of passing such a law earlier recommended by the Malimath Committee. One wishes that such a decision was taken much earlier.

There has been politicization of terror. Police feel demoralized as they are subjected to unfair and malicious criticisms, whenever they nab Hindu or Muslim terrorists. Only through martyrdom, ATS Chief Hemant Karkare and his colleagues could prove that police officers fighting against organized terror deserve support and consideration and not unfair and motivated criticisms.

It is good to see that at last some accountability has been fixed. The Home Minister and some of the bureaucrats have been axed. His resignation should have come much earlier. He was neither able to inspire confidence nor able to enthuse the officers by any kind of bold leadership.

The Prime Minister in his address to the nation has said that structural reforms in the police have to be brought about on a priority basis. Repeated terrorist attacks and the increasing crescendo of violence send a clear message that our police have become unprofessional and thoroughly politicized and will be unable to cope with the mounting internal security threats from within and without. A paradigm shift in the management of State police force is necessary. The government must carry out without any further delay the Supreme Court's directives in Prakash Singh case to adopt measures to insulate the police from extraneous pressures.

One need not be a Cassandra to prophesy that more vicious terrorists attacks are in the offing. Indeed, one can say that they have become inevitable. The success of the deadly assaults by a handful of terrorists, who could paralyze Mumbai for nearly 60 hours would hearten other Al Qaida fedayeens to launch similar assaults in future. Delhi, Bangalore and Gujarat are some of the places where deadly terrorists attacks are very likely. Country's nuclear installations are under real threat and one does not know what kind of security cover has been provided to them. Holes in our security arrangements may prompt terrorists to target the nuclear installations with catastrophic consequences. Analysis of terrorists attacks shows that often there are repeat attacks in quick succession and, hence, time is the essence and country's security apparatus has to be revamped and reinvigorated without any further delay. The new Home Minister, Shri Chidambaram, faces a stupendous challenge. There is no time to lose.

Moreover, Pakistan remains the fountainhead of Jihadi terrorism and a clear policy of dealing with Pakistan based and Pakistan trained terrorists has to be worked out. The calculation of Lakshar-I-Toyba, behind this attack is to provoke India to move troops to Pakistan border and give Pakistan army an opportunity to shift its troops locked in conflict with Al Qaida and Taliban from the western to eastern border. This will enable Al Qaida and Taliban to consolidate themselves in the Federal Administered Tribal Area (FATA) of Pakistan. New Delhi should not walk into the trap of creating a major Indo-Pakistan tension that will suit the Jihadis.

There is utmost need for intelligence coordination and an integrated internal security structure. Here, India has to draw lessons from the working of the Homeland Security of USA, where since 9/11, despite best efforts by Al Qaida and its sympathizers, no extremist attacks have taken place. Some change of tactics to encounter terrorist operations has also to be considered.

The attack on Mumbai can be a transformative moment if it strengthens nation's resolve to fight a bitter and no-holds-barred war against terror and also to adopt a slew of measures to improve our security apparatus and de-politicize the police through police reforms.

36

National Investigating Agency – Will it be an Effective Tool to Combat Terror?

After Mumbai carnage, with a rare display of unity among the political parties, the Indian parliament passed two important bills - The National Investigating Agency (NIA) Bill, 2008 and Unlawful Activities (Prevention) Amendment Bill, 2008. The statement of objects and reasons of the NIA bill states that *"over the past several years, India has been the victim of large scale terrorism sponsored from across the border..........There have been innumerable instances of terrorism across the borders and a large number of incidents have complex, inter state and international linkages. Keeping all these in view, it has been felt that there is need for setting up of an agency at the Central level for investigation of offences related to terrorism and certain other acts which have national ramifications."*

Creation of such a national agency has been in the minds of many for a long time. Several experts and committees in their reports had earlier made recommendations for establishing such an agency. The committee on Reforms of Criminals Justice System (Malimath Committee) strongly urged in favour of passing a central law for constituting a federal agency with all India character to deal with crimes that affect national security and seek to destabilize the country politically and economically. It has also been of the clear view that creation of a federal agency should not preclude state agencies from taking cognizance of such crimes. The Report says "*the state agencies and the central agency can have concurrent jurisdiction. However, if the federal agency takes up the case for investigation, the state agencies' role in the investigation of the case would automatically abate. The state agencies could also refer complicated cases to the federal agency.*"

NIA is to be entrusted with the investigation and prosecution of offences falling under *Anti-Hijacking Act 1982, Safety of Civil Aviation Act, Atomic Energy Act 1962, Unlawful Activities (Prevention) Act 1967, the Weapons of Mass Destruction and their Delivery System Act 2005, SAARC Convention on Suppression of Terrorism Act and Offences Against the State Act* mentioned in the Chapter VI of the Indian Penal Code.

Some of the important features of the newly created NIA are that, the act will be applicable to the whole of India, citizens of India outside India and persons on ships and aircrafts registered in India. The officers of NIA will have all powers, privileges and liabilities that the police officers have in connection with investigation of any offence. Whenever the central government finds that the case is terror-related, it shall direct the NIA to investigate. However, provisions of the Act with regard to investigation, shall not affect the power of state government to investigate and prosecute any terror crime or any other offences. The Act also provides that the Centre shall constitute special courts for trial of terror-related offences.

The constitution of a federal agency investigating crimes with interstate and international dimensions, was a felt need. In USA, the Federal Bureau of Investigation (FBI) is entrusted with the investigation and prosecution of offences that affect the security of the country. The list of federal crimes in the

USA investigated by FBI, includes, offences like money laundering, interstate drug trafficking, terrorism, trafficking in human being, etc.

It is heartening that the central government has taken initiative to create a federal investigating agency. Though the concept is excellent, the fact of the matter is that the new agency will take time to develop and become really effective and functional. Selection of officers, setting up of offices, sorting out of administrative tangles will take time. The country, however, is on fire. More terrorists attacks are just not likely but appear inevitable. The US think tank Rank Cooperation, in its report, has warned India of more 26/11 type attacks. The report said that India is likely to remain a target of Pakistan based terrorists, because among other things, of its inability to compel Pakistan to dismantle its terrorist infra-structure.

It would have been better and more prudent if the government enlarged the mandate of the CBI with necessary legislation and provided it with greater wherewithal to take up this responsibility. The Malimath Committee had earlier recommended that the Central Bureau of Investigation should be entrusted with the responsibility of investigating federal crimes. In the case of *Prakash Singh vs. Government of India*, the Supreme Court received materials from the National Human Rights Commission, the Bureau of Police Research and Development and the second Administrative Reforms Commission, of the need and scope of the National Investigating Agency. The NHRC clearly stated that the CBI should be entrusted with the responsibility of investigating federal crimes. The government, however, did not heed to the considered views of these expert bodies.

Section 3 (2) of the Act provides that the NIA has the power to investigate throughout India any offences noted in the attached schedule. However, NIA has no role in the prevention of the enumerated offences. In counter-terrorist operations, intelligence is the king. NIA should have a strong intelligence wing to gather, process and coordinate the inflow of relevant information. By way of example, the FBI was significantly re-structured after 9/11, so that it could engage in and collaborate with other counter-intelligence activities. NIA Act is silent on intelligence sharing and NIA's relationship with other agencies that primarily gather intelligence. Indeed, the deficiency may affect NIA's ability to investigate and prevent scheduled offences. The Mumbai tragedy exposed the deplorable lack of coordination among the multiple security agencies. It was a case where, as a security expert aptly put it, every individual and agency has all the materials to defend itself but collectively little to defend the nation.

In USA, the Department of Home Land Security was created to combat terror and the various security organizations were amalgamated among its four divisions – Border and Transportation security, Emergency preparedness and response, Chemical, Biological and Nuclear counter measures. The emphasis was on unification. Unfortunately, here we are trading the path of diversification. The NIA as an investigation agency, will succeed only when it will be supported by other existing agencies like the Intelligence Bureau and the Central Bureau of Investigation Enforcement and Directorate.

Moreover, NIA for successful functioning will require full cooperation and support of the state agencies. Indeed, this is *sine qua non.* Some of the state Chief Ministers are feeling miffed and fearing that it may be used by the central government to subserve its political ends. Section 4(1) of the Act states that "*superintendence*" of the agency shall rest with the central government without actually defining and making clear, what the superintendence really means. The failure to define superintendence in Police Acts, both at the center and state, has permitted the political bosses to interfere unabashedly in the day to day functioning of the police and erode its autonomy. It is felt that the decision, whether an offence warrants NIA involvement, should rest with the Director General NIA and not the political executives. This will lessen the scope for illegitimate political interference.

NIA, for successfully functioning will require full cooperation and support of the state police agencies. Indeed, to fight terrorism effectively, as has been done in Punjab, Andhra Pradesh and Tripura, successful strategy has been to build up the strength of the local police and the local intelligence resources. Ultimately, as the Home Minister admitted, the local *thana* is the best source for collection of intelligence. The need of the hour is to better train and equip the local police forces, expand their budgets and motivate them. US security officials in their testimonies to the Senate Committee have said that India's response to the Mumbai terrorist attack was hamstrung by lack of coordination between the different levels of the government and due to local police's inadequate training and lack of powerful weapons.

37

Communalization of Terror

Minority Affairs Minister AR Antulay created a storm by stating in the Parliament that Maharashtra Anti-Terrorists Squad (ATS) Chief Hemant Karkare was not perhaps killed by the terrorists and insinuated that there was a conspiracy to eliminate Karkare and his two colleagues. The Home Minister Chidambaram's subsequent statement in the Parliament made clear that there was no truth, whatsoever, in the suspicion of a conspiracy behind the killing of Karkare. Earlier, Karkare's role in the investigation of Malegaon blast case was questioned by BJP, Shiv Sena and now, after his death, questions had been raised by the fundamentalist elements of minority groups, regarding the circumstances in which he was killed. Chidambaram rightly said that *"both are wrong and deplorable."*

Antulay's words were lapped up by Pakistan's media as gospel truth and used to bash India for deliberately finger pointing at Pakistan for Mumbai carnage. Antulay has now become a poster boy for fundamentalist Muslim organizations. His political grand standing, meant to please his Muslim constituency, has the consequence of dividing the society on the question of fighting against terror by purveying wrong and false notions.

Antulay episode, however, goes to show, how the battle against terror has been communalized and the despicable role the politicians are playing for the sake of vote bank politics. The resultant demoralization of the police officers and men, who are in the front line of the battle against terror, is not taken note of.

In the Malegaon bomb blast case, when ATS of Maharashtra police arrested members of Abhinav Bharat, a right wing ultra Hindu group, including Sadhvi Pragya and Lt. Col. Purohit, BJP and Shiv Sena created a ruckus. They calumniated Karkare and made allegations of torture and barbaric treatment of Sadhvi Pragya by the police. Karkare was hauled over the coals and police investigation was decried as "*sinister campaign*", to destroy the reputation of individuals and tarnish the image of BJP and Shiv Sena. Both these groups even threatened to organize a *bundh*. Karkare's martyrdom during the Mumbai terror attack silenced his critics.

Similarly during the police encounter with the terrorists at Batla House in Jamia Nagar in New Delhi in which police inspector Sharma was killed, there were allegations against the police for staging fake encounters. Local politicians and human rights purists all jumped in the fray and there was a full throated cry for a judicial enquiry against the officials involved in the encounter. Even a senior congress minister on electoral considerations raised the demand for judicial enquiry. The Prime Minister very correctly and appropriately turned it down. False encounter case against Delhi Police has been dismissed by the National Human Rights Commission.

It is very unfortunate that political and electoral considerations are standing in the way of difficult, complex and time-consuming investigations against organized and determined terrorist groups. Police officers, in-charge of operations and investigations, are needlessly dragged into controversies, making their task difficult and thankless. Allegations of ultra Hindu groups that Malegaon bomb blast is nothing but a frame-up lacks credibility. It is common sense that without some clear and concrete evidence, the police would not have launched such a wide-ranging investigation covering a number of states. Again, the evidence gathered by the police would be scrutinized by the courts by going through the case diaries and police records. Any interrogation, search and arrest is called to question on communal grounds.

Similarly, the conspiracy theory behind Karkare's death is far-fetched and outcome of a febrile imagination. It has been exploited by Pakistan in its game of denial and deliberate refusal to initiate any action against the perpetrators of Mumbai carnage. The police operations against terrorists outfits in the country like SIMI, HUJI are getting hobbled because, very often, they are charged with anti-Muslim bias. This makes it difficult for the police to function boldly and vigorously. The hard fact to be taken note of is that the Islamic Jihadi groups have been able to establish their own modules in different parts of the country. Many of these groups enjoy committed local Muslim support. Without such support, strikes launched by some of these groups, would not have been possible. This does not mean that the entire Muslim community should be viewed with suspicion and profiled as terrorists. Any inappropriate stereotyping of the minority community will be a terrible mistake. Nevertheless, utmost police vigilance against the organizations working in Indian soil and sucked in the global whirls of jihad is called for. Collusion of some local Muslims with the jihadis has widened the scope and magnitude of the terrorists' threats in the country.

Police counter-terrorist operations should be periodically reviewed to ensure that the police function within the bounds of law and innocent persons do not come to grief. This will alienate the police from the support and cooperation of the minority community That is the lesson to be drawn from the enforcement of the TADA in the nineties. Courts and review bodies have to ensure, that the police operate within the four corners of law. But in counter-terrorist operations, the police must enjoy a certain amount of operational independence and flexibility. Otherwise, they will be neither successful nor effective. To hamstring the police operations by communalizing terror is bound to be counter-productive. It will have an adverse effect on police morale and diminish their zeal to vigorously combat the ruthless Jihadi terrorists by risking their lives.

The Parliament has now passed Unlawful Activities (Prevention) Amendment Act, 2008, to provide more teeth in the existing anti-terror laws. Unfortunately, confession before the police under this Act is not admissible. This has been perhaps done with a view to allaying the fears of the minority communities and showing that the new Act is not a replication of POTA. With certain safeguards, confession before a senior police officer, should have been made admissible (as was recommended by the Malimath Committee in its report on Criminal Justice Reforms) because, in cases of serious terrorist violence, many witnesses, out of fear will not come forward to depose and the prosecution, willy-nilly will have to depend upon the testimony of the police officers. In all democratic countries, confession before the police is admissible as evidence. Further, it will be difficult to gather evidence of the planning, preparation and logistics of the terrorists, if we shut out as inadmissible, confession before the police.

The term "*Hindu terrorists*" and "*Muslim terrorists*" are being loosely used by the media and political leaders. This will only go to broaden the constituency of the terrorists, provide wrong notions to the common people and make the work of police more difficult. The country has to brace itself for more vicious and sinister form of terrorist violence in the coming days. To communalize the issue of terror for political considerations and gains will be a serious blunder during these testing times. It will derail the country's united stand against the scourge of terrorism.

38

Intelligence Failure

After violent terrorist strikes in Mumbai trains, killing 197 passengers and injuring more than 800, there is a shrill and loud cry of intelligence failure. Many responsible political leaders as well as members of the press have castigated the intelligence agencies and also the national security advisor, for failure to provide timely and precise intelligence to alert the police and other security agencies of the strike plans of the Jihadi terrorists. The criticisms though understandable, are not however very fair or correct.

Collection of intelligence about the plans and operations of the well-organised terrorist outfits is an extremely difficult and challenging job. It requires careful planning and long preparation. Modern terrorists do not constitute one single homogeneous group. They are divided into several small centrifugal groups and penetration into one group may not throw light on the activities of other groups. Different modus operandi of the terrorist groups the wide range of potential threats, random nature of attacks and absence of discernible Standard Operating Procedures (SOPs), make it difficult to get reliable advance warning about terrorist attacks. Normally, there are few Early Warning Indicators (EWIs).

Modern terrorist groups also devise elaborate anti-infiltration procedures and take steps to ruthlessly weed out informers from their ranks. It is a hard fact that covert human intelligence (Humanist) is the most useful source of information about the terrorists. Sometimes, operations have to be mounted on agent's words alone and that is the only source of information, one has to rely on. But raising a source in place and then handling him successfully is a difficult and time-consuming job, which requires elaborate preparation. There are no instant successes.

It must be said to the credit of the police and intelligence agencies that they have been able to foil planned strikes of the terrorists in Nagpur and other places in Maharashtra and recover large caches of smuggled arms and RDX. Thus, though failures of intelligence agencies are trumpeted, their success go unheralded. However, it was inevitable that some of the terrorist groups would be able to break through the ring and launch further strikes.

According to police investigators, the Mumbai train blasts was a joint operation of Lashkar-i-Toiba, a Kashmiri separatist group that has been outlawed since 2002 in Pakistan, and the banned Students Islamic Movement of India (SIMI), a home-grown Jihadi outfit, that is spreading its tentacles among the disaffected Muslims across the country. The two organisations are united in the cause of bringing the entire subcontinent under the Muslim rule.

Lashkar-i-Toiba and SIMI partnership have been growing for many years and the two groups collaborated on the bombing of New Delhi markets as well as bomb attacks on Varanasi temples. Though the Government of India banned SIMI in 2001, yet it continues to grow and may have 500 hardcore members and 20000 sympathisers, who can be relied upon for assistance and shelter. With SIMI support, Lashkar fighters can now operate inside India without a lifeline to Pakistani side of the border. SIMI has been reportedly receiving funds from Riyadh-based World Assembly of Muslim Youth and is also morally and financially supported by Chicago based Consultative Committee of Indian Muslims (CIM). Further, it has managed to keep its network alive through clandestine activities and pseudonymous fronts and organisations.

Thus, though Pakistan remains the epicentre of India-specific terrorism, the hard fact has to be acknowledged that Laskhar-i-toiba, India's most potent security threat, has now been able to establish elaborate network inside the country, with local recruits like Simi. In cities like Mumbai, Delhi and other places, SIMI has safe houses and extensive network of fund managers, who transfer arms, explosives and money for the use of the terrorists.

It is estimated that at least 100 people participated in the execution of Mumbai bomb blasts. Without committed local Muslim support, such well-organised strikes would not have been possible. According to intelligence estimates, there are a number of organisations working on Indian soil to breed a sense of alienation among the Muslim youths and suck them into the global whirl of Jihad. The collusion of the local Muslims with the global Jihadis enlarges the scope and magnitude of terrorist threats in the country. It is necessary to disabuse our minds of the facile assumption that Muslims in India have not responded to Jihadi ideology because of our democratic ethos and syncretic culture.

The need of the hour is a no-holds barred policy of firmly and ruthlessly dealing with the militants, with a view to dismantling the networks they have built up in different areas of the country. In these counter-terrorist operations, the intelligence outfits have to play a crucial role. Unfortunately, police intelligence apparatuses in most of the states are in a bad shape. They are now packed with people, who lack professional expertise and have been picked up on considerations other than competence. There is substance in the complaint that they are mainly used for political surveillances, collection of intelligence regarding intra-party and inter-party problems. Further, even when hard intelligence is available, follow-up action is not taken on considerations of vote bank politics. The DMK Government, barely two weeks after coming to power, ordered dropping of cases against 12 Muslim fundamentalists, involved in Coimbtore serial blasts. This blatant display of sympathy for Muslim fundamentalists is mainly due to electoral considerations.

Further, state police forces have become completely politicised and incapable of acting freely and independently due to constant extraneous pressures and considerations. Powers that-be, have always shied away from meaningful structural reforms in the police. But in these testing times, police force should be allowed to function decisively without interference and police leaders should be given a free hand and operational independence.

Again, there should be stiff anti-terrorist laws. Early this year, the U.S. Congress passed the draconian anti-terrorist law, U.S. Patriot Act. The Patriot Act allows intelligence and law-enforcement agencies to go into places of worship, investigate the working of charities and scoop on tele-communication of the suspects. Some of the provisions, can be, and have been misused. But anti-terrorist laws should not be scrapped, because they have been misused in some instances. Steps have to be taken to see that law enforcers, who misused the provisions of stringent laws, are appropriately punished. Further, it is necessary to make the people aware of the magnitude and dimensions of the terrorist threat and steps that should be taken, to counteract it. The key to success in anti-terrorist campaigns in a democracy is a public, sensitised to and aware of terrorist goals and supportive of needed counter-terrorist measures by the government.

As Jihadi terrorism has already made its home in India and can surface at any time in any place, India's internal security, has to be really strengthened and galvanised. India can draw lessons from the working of the Homeland security in USA. where, since 9/11, not a single terrorist attack has taken place. The Department of Homeland Security, with a variety of alert measures and drills, have ensured that since 9/11, there has been, despite many efforts by Al-Quaida and its sympathisers, no terrorist attack in USA. It is true that even with the best of effects, some terrorist strikes cannot be prevented. The Israeli intelligence and police services are probably the best in the world when it comes to counter-terrorist operations. Even then, cities like Tel Aviv and Haifa are successfully targeted by the suicide bombers. But no efforts should be spared to put as much heat on the terrorists as possible and make their operations really difficult.

It is a fact that Pakistan is aiding and abetting cross-border terrorism with a view to making India bleed. It continues, despite constant denials, to run training camps for the terrorists. Recently, a senior analyst of U.S. Department of Defence, has told the trial court in California that the examination of certain satellite images in the remote Balakot terrain in Pakistan, indicates a strong probability of existence of militant training camps there. This has also been corroborated by a Pakistani American terrorist, arrested in California. India now has to firmly tell USA that, it cannot consider Pakistan as an ally in the war against terror when the same Pakistan continues to shelter terrorists in its soil. It is true that US needs the Pakistan army to help it against Al-qaida in Afghan border, but the Pakistan army needs the USA even more. American support and cooperation with Pakistan should be conditional on verifiable good behaviour on all fronts.

However, the fact to be borne in mind is that the US pressures may not very much force *Musharaff* to go for a real crack down on the Jihadi fundamentalists. Laskar, which was banned by Musharaff in 2002, has now resurfaced as Jammat-ud-Dawat, a Muslim aid Organisation. Jammat played a significant role in assisting Pakistani Kashmiris in the wake of last October's devastating earthquake. Because of domestic compulsions, *Musharaff* cannot go for a violent confrontation with Pakistan's religious right. The unfortunate fact looming large is that Pakistan is becoming a bigoted place and fast hurtling towards an "*Islamist edge*."

The view of the moderate elements in Pakistan is that the best way to undercut radicalism is continuation of dialogues between India and Pakistan, despite terror blasts. Peace processes will strengthen the moderate forces in Pakistan, rather than heavy-handed offensive against the Jihadi elements. At the same time, some change of tactics in counter-terrorist operations, has to be considered. During *Intifida*, Israel's army developed new techniques for low-intensity conflicts and concluded that one of the effective strategies is to kill the rebel leaders. Assassination, relying heavily on intelligence, became a feature of counter-terrorist operations. It did have a sobering impact on the Palestinian militants.

39

Torture: Is There Any Justification?

Torture, which constitutes one of the most heinous violation of human rights, has become a global problem. Torture has been defined in the Tokyo Declaration, 1975, by the World Medical Association as a "*deliberate systematic and wanton infliction of physical or mental suffering by one or more persons acting alone or on the order of any authority to force another person to yield information or to make a confession*". Torture is no longer an "*indigenous activity*". It has become international. Foreign experts, as Amnesty International's report mentions, are sent from one country to another to explain and demonstrate the methods of torture. Modern torture equipments are also exported from one country to the other. In short, what has been a historical curiosity has developed a life of its own and become a social cancer.

Torture is a crime under international law. International standards, such as Geneva Conventions, UN Convention against Torture and the International Covenant on Civilian and Political Rights, ban torture or any kind of cruel, inhuman, degrading treatment even in times of war. The ban is absolute. UN Convention Against Torture (1984) provides that each state shall take effective, legal, administrative, judicial and other measures to prevent acts of torture and no exceptional circumstances, whether a state of war or internal political instability or any public emergency, may be invoked as a justification of torture. To date, 144 countries have ratified the Convention against Torture. India did not accede to the convention for a long time, despite repeated urgings of the National Human Rights Commission. In a letter (9th December 1994) addressed to the Prime Minister, the Chairman, National Human Rights Commission stated that in this year of 125th anniversary of the birth of Mahatma Gandhi, the Republic could best pay tribute to the values he embodied by acceding to the 1984 Convention Against Torture and other forms of Cruel, Inhuman and Degrading Treatment or Punishment. The Commission also refuted the apprehensions of the government that acceding to the Convention will open the country to interference from outside. Though the Government of India at last signed the Convention against Torture, 1997, it has not so far ratified it, despite repeated reminders of the National Human Rights Commission and other human rights groups. India is now in the company of countries like Sudan, North Korea, Zimbabwe and Myanmar that have not ratified the Convention. The right against torture has been judicially recognized as a fundamental right by the Supreme court of the country and, hence, this delay in ratification is embarrassing for the country and inexplicable to those, who are interested in better promotion of human rights.

Now with the commencement of the war against terror after 9/11, attempts are being made to justify torture under certain exceptional circumstances. There are exponents of the view that torture is permissible under certain circumstances in the war against terrorism. Some lawyers and academics uphold the view that torture can be justified in some rare cases. A notable exponent of this view is Alen Dreshowitz, a leading

American criminal defence lawyer. He has argued for "*torture warrants*" in cases of "*ticking bomb*" urgency. In practice, however, attempts to use torture sparingly have only led to widespread abuse. Historical practice shows that there is no such thing as little bit of torture to compel someone to speak during an interrogation. Once a certain degree of force is permitted, interrogators face an overwhelming temptation to apply as much force as they consider necessary to acquire the sought-for information. There is always the difficulty of knowing where to draw the line and one cannot rely on interrogators to bear in mind such distinctions. It is the danger of "*slippery slope*" that makes opponents of torture insist on total ban.

Israel is the only country in modern times that has allowed "*moderate physical pressure*" as a last resort. But in 1999, the Supreme Court of Israel, citing the slippery slope argument ruled that torture could never be justified even in the case of a ticking bomb. The court went to the extent of outlawing techniques such as sleep deprivation, exposure to extremes of hot and cold, prolonged stress positions and violent shaking. In 1970s, when Britain used similar techniques against the suspected terrorists of Northern Ireland, those were banned by the European Court of Human Rights, following a case brought by the Republic of Ireland.

In a BBC survey of 27000 people in 25 countries in 2008, it was found that large number of people in many countries, including, America consider a degree of torture acceptable, if it saves lives. Another poll by PEW Research Centre found that nearly half of all Americans thought that torture of suspected terrorists was sometimes justified.

In the war against terror, while President Bush had condemned torture, legal officers of US government issued notorious "*torture memos*" that sought to restrict definition of torture to serious physical injury, organ failure or even death. It describes certain forms of ill treatment as "*stress and distress technique*" and claimed that certain forms of ill treatment are not necessarily illegal and can be justified on grounds of military necessity or self-defence. But torture or ill-treatment do not become permissible by being euphemistically called something else. It was held in the memo that as the wartime commander-in-chief entrusted with the responsibility of saving the lives of American people, the American President has the power to override both domestic and international law. Most of these memos, after being leaked in 2004, were withdrawn.

In respect of the suspects held at Guantanamo Bay, the American Supreme Court in 2006, did not accept the plea of the administration that detainees were foreigners and the Guantanamo Bay was beyond the reach of the American courts. The Supreme Court ruled in "*Hamdan*" case that all the detainees, wherever, held were protected by the common article of the Geneva Conventions, which bans torture as well as all other kinds of degrading, cruel and inhuman treatment. Nevertheless, for enhanced interrogation, of terrorist suspects, the CIA is carrying out extraordinary "*rendition of suspects*" to clandestine prisons in third world countries. Initially, the programme's existence was not officially confirmed until President Bush announced transfer of 14 hardcore detainees, to Guantanamo who were held in "*black sites*" around the world. According to Human Rights Watch that, of the 100 suspected terrorists believed to have been surrendered over past 6 years, as many as 39 have remained unaccounted. It is alleged that countries, which are known to practice torture, have been specifically selected to receive "*war on terror detainees for interrogation.*" This, indeed, amounts to "*outsourcing*" torture. The USA was one of the principal architects behind the adoption in 1948 of the Universal Declaration of Human Rights, which forms the basis of today's body of international human rights law. But many of its actions in the present war on terror amounts to rejection of the standards, which it so often says it expects of others.

Use of torture and ill treatment does undermine the process of justice since international human rights law prohibits information obtained as a result of torture in any legal proceedings. In many countries, the prohibition is reflected in domestic law. In 2004, Britain's Courts of Appeals ruled that information acquired through torture is admissible as evidence in the court. But the ruling was later overturned by the House of Lords.

However, despite legal ban, torture continues because authorities in many countries have not taken a tough and unambiguous stand against it. Further, as Michel Ignatief, a Canadian writer, has said. Besides extraction of vital information torture is also motivated by the baser instincts of inflicting pain, exacting revenge or even for fun. This seems to have happened in many prisons and torture camps like Abu Gharib.

40

Perspectives on Police Violence

It is reported in the press that two police personnel responsible for brutally thrashing a petty criminal at Bhagalpur and then tying his leg to a motorcycle and dragging him in the road have been departmentally punished. The constable has already been dismissed and the recommendations for the dismissal of the Assistant Sub-Inspector of police has been made by the state police headquarters to the government. They will also face criminal prosecution.

Disturbing images of this act of police violence and barbarity telecast nationwide have shocked the public conscience. The National Human Rights Commission and the National Commission for Minorities, which called for reports from the Bihar police authorities, will perhaps now close the case as the defaulting policemen have got their just desserts. But prompt punishment of the errant policemen will touch the surface of the problem. The wider issues of the systemic cause of police violence and deviance have to be addressed. This deep seated malady afflicting the police force in the country requires a close and hard look.

Efforts are sometimes made to explain away grotesque misuse of police force, by characterizing the offenders as a few rotten apples. This view is too simplistic. Abuse and misuse of force by the police is decidedly more complex and multidimensional than the few bad apples theory would imply. Maurice Punch in a perceptive study "*Conduct Unbecoming*" states, that the roots of police deviance are "*deep seated and results from, as noticed in different countries of the world, improper legislation, occupational culture and desire to produce quick results*". Officer's personality features represent only one element of the problem. Police deviance is symptomatic of a deep system-wide problem. Organizational culture and practices are very often responsible for police misconduct.

In fact, police violence and brutality are correlated to thc public regard for the police authority. Lower public regard reduces police self-esteem, thereby making use of force more likely. On the other hand, unwarranted use of force lowers public regard for the police. Therefore, other things being equal, one finds higher incidence of force in countries, where the police are poorly regarded than where they enjoy better public respect. In countries like Japan and UK, where the police enjoy public regard, there are few occasions of lethal use of force. But the situation is not so in countries like India or USA where public regard for the police is uncertain, if not brittle.

The incidence of use of force also varies with the social distance between the police and the members of the public. There is evidence to show, that police aggression is often directed at persons, who have a marginal position in society, elements who dwell on the fringes of respectability like racial minorities or moral lepers like homosexuals and alcoholics. They become special targets of police aggression and are called "*Police Properties*". This problem is faced by the police forces in many countries of the world.

It is also seen that police violence and excessive use of force is restricted in societies, where *reserve* and physical restraint are valued. This is a cultural variable. Professor David Bayley points out that in Japan, a policeman, who forebodes the use of force, even at the risk of physical and emotional repression, is respected for being so. By contrast, an American policeman considers backing down as cowardly. Again, the use of force and authority by the police, is also influenced by societal factors, that vary from country to country. In a country like Japan, where police contacts with the citizens are less confrontational and police penetration of the community more low-key or routine; there are few occasions of misuse of force by the police against the citizens. But in India, where police contact with the citizens, mainly takes place in adversarial situations, a wall of mistrust remains between them. The relationship remains confrontational.

Again, the police behaviour and internal discipline is powerfully influenced by the vocational sense that personnel bring to their work. If policing is viewed as a calling and not just a job with pay and retirement benefits, the standard of internal discipline will be higher. The police in Japan and UK have developed a much greater sense of vocation than police in India or USA.

Lynch Justice

In the Bhagalpur case, the police violence was supported by the public. The same was the story of the blindings of the criminals that had taken place earlier at Bhagalpur. The loss of public faith in the criminal justice system has encouraged this ominous trend of lynch justice. Many instances are coming to notice, of people taking laws in their own hands or prevailing upon the police to resort to extra legal violent methods. Thus, abuses of authority by the police can flourish not only because of official negligence or acquiescence, but because many people, rightly or wrongly approve of it as an unpleasant and unavoidable necessity.

Conscientious police officers, particularly, police leaders, have to check drift of this kind. They have to bear in mind that in any democratic society, order maintained through repression is the worst form of disorder. It establishes a linkage between social order and atrocity. If the police can learn to submerge the short term considerations of the use of force, in favour of long-term considerations of professional prestige, they may find their use of force less necessary and less controversial. As the Director of the National Police Academy, I often used to tell the IPS probationers that the police officers are accountable to law and have to function within its four corners. There is no scope for counter violence under the Indian Penal Code.

Training Intervention

Proper and well-conducted violence reduction training programmes can have some effect in influencing conduct and reflexes of the police officers. Bad temper and proclivity towards violence can be successfully reduced by training. Maintaining one's temper under stressful conditions, is a skill that can be taught. There is also need to build a climate of opinion in the organization that frowns upon unnecessary display of authority and excessive use of violence by the police. Mere sanctions against some errant officers and men, for using violence inappropriately, will not help.

The influence of organization in shaping the behaviour and responses of the members is far-reaching. In the annals of police, there is the example of building up of a police organization, with a new code of ethics and behaviour. The first two commissioners of Robert Peel's London Metropolitan Police, were able through ceaseless vigilance, to raise a police force, which was unarmed and committed to eschew violence as far as possible. The success of British police was dramatic and had a permanent impact on the public attitude towards the police and the use of force by the police. This is so because the police, whether they recognize it or not are important social actors, who influence public attitudes on law, government and use of force.

41

Custody Deaths

Cases of deaths in police custody have embroiled Delhi Police in controversies and given it a lot of adverse publicity. Indeed, custodial death invariably does irretrievable damage to the police and blackens its reputation. In the words of the Supreme Court "Custodial violence is a calculated assault on human dignity and whenever human dignity is wounded, civilization takes a step backward. The flag of humanity in each occasion must fly half mast" (DK Basu Vs. The State of West Bengal). These are indeed soul stirring words.

Various orders and instructions have been issued by the Supreme Court and also by the National Human Rights Commission from time to time to curb custodial violence by the police. But the success achieved so far has been limited. The National Human Rights Commission immediately after its formation in 1993, had issued directions to the District Magistrates and Superintendents of Police of all states in the country to report within 24 hours all cases of death in both police and jail custody. In a number of cases, where custodial deaths were due to torture or police high handedness, NHRC's investigation wing investigated into the cases and NHRC recommended in a number of cases, action against the aberrant staff as well as compensation to the victims. However, there has been just marginal improvement in the situation. In 2003-2004, there were instances of 167 deaths in police custody and in 2004-2005 (till January) 112 cases were reported. Earlier, there was high incidence of custodial deaths in states like Bihar and UP. But now, a number of cases are being reported from Gujarat and Maharashtra and in other states, not affected earlier.

Hence, the question as to why custodial violence, by and large, continues unabated calls for a close examination. Custodial violence and torture are not new phenomena in India. The Commission for Investigation of Torture in Madras Presidency (commonly referred to as the Torture Commission) in its report stated (1850) that police torture was quite prevalent in the then Madras Presidency. The Indian Police Commission (1902-1903) had also mentioned about the "unnecessary severity with which the police officers perform their duty". The National Police Commission also, in its first report (1979) analyzed the scourge of custodial deaths and rape and suggested a number of corrective measures, including, mandatory judicial enquiries.

Custodial deaths generate more heat than light. The assumption that custodial deaths occur just because police officers are sadists and violence prone is an erroneous one. The causes are more serious and complex. Corrective strategies, if they are to be successful, must take note of them. First, there is tremendous pressure on the police to detect cases whenever there is a surge in crime, particularly, violent crime. The popular impression is that, efficiency or inefficiency of the police is the determining factor behind any such upswing in crime. The pressure is felt more by the subordinate staff, who are required to deliver the result in quick time. They resort to short cut third degree methods to achieve their ends. Custodial deaths often occur, not because of any intention to kill the victim but as a result of excessive torture, or when quite unknowingly the officer injures some weak organ in a victim's anatomy. Second, because of the slow judicial process and malfunctioning of the criminal justice system, the public also expect the police to take law in their own hands and see that the criminals get their just desserts. Because of incompatible demands of the public, some policemen become stoically immune to criticisms. Police officers and even political leaders, instead of resisting such pressures, succumb to them. Third, the political bosses often wink at police violence and excesses to serve their own partisan political ends. They misuse the police and create in them a culture of impunity. This has severely weakened the chain of command, eroded accountability and encouraged corruption. And corruption in police, impairs life and liberty of the citizens and encourages criminality. The Chief of Police today has very little say in the transfer and posting of officers, which is being controlled by the Chief Minister or Home Minister. I know of cases, where the Chief Minister advised the Superintendents of Police, not to bother about the human rights abuses by the subordinate police staff, so long as they play the ball. That is the reason, why political parties of all hues, are totally opposed to structural reforms in police to insulate it from extraneous influence and interference. Fourth, in very few cases of custodial deaths or violence, culpable officers get punishment. Whenever such incidents occur, there is a public outcry. The officers are either transferred or suspended and disciplinary action or criminal prosecutions commence, but in the long run, very few officers get punished. It will be an interesting study to find out, in how many cases during 1999-2004 in some of the states rocked by custodial violence, officers were held guilty and adequately punished.

In the case of DK Basu Vs State of West Bengal, the Supreme Court has laid down mandatory guidelines for dealing with persons kept in police custody. The National Police Commission has recommended mandatory judicial enquiries in all cases of custodial death and this viewpoint was endorsed by the NHRC. But things have not improved, because no sustained effort has been made to foster a human rights culture within the police and make the police officers realise that even from a practical point of view, adherence to human rights norms will enable them to do their jobs better. Custodial torture and violence are counter-productive and expose the police to public condemnation and criminal prosecution.

Some egregious cases of custodial death and torture wash away all the good and hard work done by the police and create a strong negative impression in public mind. Moreover, the police are scapegoated for the failure of other agencies of the criminal justice system.

Again, in every police outfit, there are some violence prone officers, who figure again and again in cases of misuse and abuse of force. Unfortunately, regarding these aggressive and violence prone officers very little empirical study has been done in India. In USA, Christopher Commission looked into the use of force (1991) by Los Angeles Police after the Rodney Kind incident. It pinpointed, by going through the records of Los Angeles Police Department, a number of officers against whom there were repeated allegations of misuse of force. They were encouraged by the aggressive style of law enforcement of Los Angeles Police. There should be no hesitation on the part of police leaders to discipline and weed out such black sheep from the force. This calls for solidarity against and not on behalf of these aggressive officers. Further, it has been found that a police officer is more likely to resort to violence and excesses when there are other officers to provide physical and psychological reinforcements.

Proper and well conducted training interventions can influence the conduct and reflexes of the police officers and reduce bad temper and proclivity towards violence. Also constant exhortation demostrated by as many upright officers to the members of the force at cutting edge levels that custodial violence and torture are self defeating and expose them to punitive action.

This will have in a restraining impact and build up an organizational climate that frowns on misuse of force and other forms of excesses. External mechanisms to enhance police accountability and penalize police aberrations are necessary in a democratic society but meaningful and lasting changes in the organization can only come from within.

42

Problem Oriented Policing

Policing, despite many existing stereotypes, is an extra ordinarily complex endeavour. By the very nature of the function, the police are an anomaly in a free society. In a democratic society, as H. Goldstein puts it *"they are invested with a great deal of authority under a system of governance in which the authority is reluctantly granted, and when granted, sharply curtailed."*

Nevertheless, successful functioning of the police in a democratic society depends upon its ability to maintain a certain degree of order, without which a free society cannot function. The strength of a democratic society, the quality of life enjoyed by the citizens, are determined in a large measure by the ability of the police to discharge their duties efficiently. Further, police organisations have some of their own peculiar characteristics. Police officers, unlike Army units, are spread out in field and not subject to direct supervision. The individual officers possess awesome authority to deprive people of liberty, and even of their lives, and this authority of necessity is delegated to individuals to be exercised in most instances without proper review and control.

In western democratic countries, particularly in the USA, the prevalent professional model of policing places a high value on police being apolitical. It advocates tight discipline, efficient use of personnel and technology as well as high standards of training. However, the professional model came under enormous pressure in the late 1960s and early 70s with increase in crime, civil rights protests movements and complaints of minority groups against the police. Further, researches on police and police operations conducted during the 1970s, revealingly showed limitations of practices like random patrol, rapid response, follow-up criminal investigations that constituted the bedrocks of policing for many years.

The lessons drawn from these studies challenged the value of standard operating procedures of the police and revealed that police resources have been invested in a limited number of practices based on some simplistic concepts of the police role.

The researchers also provided some other important insights. These are:

- Police deal with a range of problems, many of which are not criminal in nature;
- Arrest and prosecution alone, traditional functions of the police, do not resolve problems;
- The police can use a variety of methods to redress the recurrent problems and design different solutions to solve them.
- Police use a wide range of methods, formal and informal, in getting the job done. Law enforcement is only one of the methods among the many.

It was Goldstein, who first coined the term "*problem oriented policing*" in 1979. He felt that professional policing only takes a very narrow view of policing and "*perpetuates the conflict between the concern for operating efficiently and concern for substance*". He views problem-oriented policing as a comprehensive plan for improving policing, in which high priority is attached to addressing substantive problems that face the police. In professional model of policing, the major emphasis is on handling incidents effectively. The efficiency of policing is judged by how speedily they solve the problem assigned to them and, thus, police officers often deal with the superficial manifestations of deeper problems. The first step in problem-oriented policing is to move beyond just handling the incidents and take a more in-depth interest by understanding and appraising the forces and factors giving rise to them. The problem, thus, becomes the unit of police work and serves as a reminder that the job of policing is much more than dealing with crime and criminal law. The police must proactively try to solve the problems rather than react to the consequences of the problem.

A crucial feature of problem oriented policing is that it seeks solutions tailored to specific problems. Arrest and law enforcement are not abandoned, but an effort is made in each situation to analyse the problem carefully and meticulously to find out which of the alternative responses are best suited for effectively dealing with the problem. The notion of choosing the tool that best suits the problem instead of grabbing the most familiar and convenient tool in the toolbox lies close to the heart of problem solving.

Goldstein advocated that police must recognise their role in society as broader than just enforcing the criminal law. At the same time, he argued, that the police mandate may not be unlimited and all encompassing. According to him, if the police become involved in every government and quasi government activities, they risk eroding the balance of power in local and national governments. Like the army, there is a sound political rationale for keeping police out of certain forms of decision-making. There is an obvious danger that the police agencies many over-extend their resources and try to achieve objectives about which they have little or no expertise.

Problem-oriented approach requires careful search for alternatives by the police. This is a legitimate enterprise, central to police functioning. The police should be dissuaded from applying a single response haphazardly to a wide range of different types of problems. But search for alternatives should be preceded by a careful analysis of the new problems of concern. Striking out in a new direction without thinking through the problem can be counter-productive and has to be discouraged.

In problem solving, the police play the role of helping the community rather than depending on police power and criminal justice system control. The police have also tried to make use of specific forms of social control inherent in existing relationships, like parents over children, and teachers over students, rather than depending on police power and authority of the criminal justice system for control. Indeed, there are enormous potentials for making greater use of the other social control mechanism. For proper management and utilization of police resources, the police have to be more outspoken. Very often the bulk of police resources are utilized in an unthinking manner for various general crime prevention assignments. The police will have to indicate to the community, the manner in which targeted response based on systematic analysis can address community problems better than current practices.

By 2000, many police agencies in Canada, U.K., Australia, New Zealand and South Africa reported that they are engaged in problem- oriented policing in some form or other; and some have made problem-oriented policing, specifically, as the focal point of their long-range strategic plans.

Some community policing experts are of the view that problem-oriented policing is a tactic, tool or method that one might use within a community policing philosophy. This view, however, fails to take note of the critical differences between community policing and a problem-oriented policing. They have different primary goals, and consequently some different methods. Moreover it reduced Goldstein's intensive and rigorous analysis of community-wide problems to a more general street or neighbourhood problem-solving. Street level problem-solving tends to focus on problems that are small in scope. Officers analyse the problems and tend to draw on personal experience for responses, which often includes enforcement in concert with one or two other agencies. It is often more thoughtful and analytical than knee-jerk law enforcement.

Lay members of the community frequently assume that the police have much more authority and capacity than they actually possess. Explaining the constraints and limitations of the police to the community will enable the community to realise the difficulties and limitations under which the police operate. This will release some of the pressure on the police and police suggestions and proposals will evoke better response from the community. In a democratic society, in which complex social problems will always place heavy demands on the police, it is necessary to strive constantly and not periodically for a form of policing that is not only effective but also humane and civil, that not only protects individual rights and other values basic to a democracy but strengthens our commitment to them.

In recent years, initiatives have been taken in many places to expand problem oriented policing programmes. Among these efforts, the work sponsored by Britain's Home Office has special significance. It introduces the situational approach - a concept that emphasizes changing the environment (rather than changing the people) and the need to concentrate on specific types of offences or locales. But problem-oriented policing requires incorporating these efforts to the mainstream of policing and making them institutionalized and also an integral part of the police management and operations.

43

Legalization of Prostitution: Myths and Realities

It is learnt that the Government of India is debating over the issue of legalization and de-criminalization of prostitution. Some feminine groups as well as human rights activists are aggressively campaigning for legalization of prostitution. Advocates of legalization hold the view that prostitution should be given the status of industry and sex work must be considered as similar to any other work. Prostitutes must be considered as legitimate sex workers. Conferences were held in Kolkata in 1997, 1998 again in 2001 demanding legalization. Many NGOs lent their support to this demand. *Sangram*, a voluntary organisation in Maharashtra, working around the prostitutes, champions the cause of prostitutes and glorifies the freedom supposed to be inherent in prostitution. Dr Syeeda Hameed, former Member of National Commission for Women, feels that "*the shame that surrounds the sex workers and illegality which brands them makes it difficult for them to seek any redress. It is necessary that they should not be treated as criminals and given rights and dignity that they deserve*[1]."

International Experience

Prostitution has been legalized in countries like Australia, Germany, New Zealand and Netherlands, etc. Brothel prostitution was legalized in Victoria in 1984, the Australian capital territory in 1992, in Queensland in 1999 and in New South Wales in 1999. The proponents of legalization have upheld Victoria and New-South-Wales models as good practices in various national and international fora. Legalization and decriminalization are viewed as providing safety to prostituted women and solutions to their health hazards.

Unfortunately, even two decades after legalization of prostitution in Victoria, there are studies that clearly reveal that this experiment has been a failure and its objectives have remained unfulfilled. In legalized brothels, the prostituted women, and not the male customers, are examined for sexually transmitted diseases on a regular basis. It is a retrograde step and marks return to a time when the state itself took a role in providing disease-free women for men's sexual pleasure. One of the primary objects of legalization has been to protect women from sexually transmitted diseases like HIV/AIDS, but studies have revealed that practices in legal brothels expose women to far greater health hazards. They face greater risks of unwanted pregnancy and sexually transmitted diseases because men often do not use condoms. A study in Victoria found that 40% of clients had enjoyed prostituted women without using condoms[2].

Safety of Women

Legalization according to its proponents ensures the safety of women in prostitution. But facts prove otherwise. Marry Sullivan's research on the Occupational Health and Safety Codes for brothels developed in Australia by state governments and prostitutes' rights organisation documents the kind of violence that exists in such industry. The OHSC code suggests that women exercise their "*intuition to work out whether the buyers are likely to be violent. But the prostituted women may be fined by their employers if they refuse to service clients, whom the women considered to be dangerous*[3]*.*"

Indeed, legalization makes men more demanding of practices, which women do not like and makes women further powerless to resist them because of greater competition. It gives more power and muscle to the brothel owners[4].

Street Prostitution

It has been argued by the proponents of legalization that it would discourage street prostitution and the street prostitutes, for safety reasons will choose to work in legal brothels. But this however, does not happen in practice. Street prostitution and problems associated with this have remained the same and sometimes have increased following legalization. Research estimates that 80% of street prostitutes in Victoria are addicts and 80 to 90% are homeless. Local councils and state governments have undertaken new legislation and initiatives to deal with this growing problem.

In New South Wales, a local council has set up "*Safe houses*" which allows women to take their male buyers picked up from the tolerance zones. But safe houses and sex workers' centers, under the control of local government, are better understood as state run brothels. Another problem with the creation of tolerance zone is that local authorities are encouraging aggressive sexual behaviour of males and their tendency to abuse women in those areas.

South Australian MP Steve Condous visited New South Wales in July, 2000, on a survey of brothels. He was shocked to find sharp increase in street prostitution-"*street prostitution had become so bad that it led to a street protest by St. Kilda residents in 2001*[5]." By contrast, Swedish law introduced on 1st January, 1999 prohibited sexual services and there is evidence that it had led to a major reduction of the prostitutes in the streets.

Increase in Organised Crime

A significant objective of legalization of prostitution is to control involvement of crime gangs in running the brothels and exploiting the prostitutes. But in reality, wherever prostitution has been legalized, the illegal sector has grown much larger than the legalized sector. In Victoria, it has been estimated by the police that the number of illegal brothels is really 400, four-times more than the legal brothels[6]. New South Wales police in 2000 reported about 40 shootings, as part of a struggle between rival groups for control of prostitution. A Dutch academic reported that in Holland the brothel trade is dominated by illegal immigrants imported by Polish and Russian Mafia[7]. It is a fact that legalization and decriminalization has accounted for the growth of prostitution industry. Legalization institutionalizes and legitimizes the sex industry pimps masquerade as "*foremen*" and "*legal enterprises*" and rationalize the marketing of prostitutes locally or transnationally.

To meet the growing demands for more sex workers, brothel keepers and other captains of sex industry resort to trafficking in women and children. Traffickers sell women to both legal and illegal brothels. Trafficked women can work legally in brothels with work permits if traffickers apply on their behalf for refugee status. Many of the trafficked women are so debt-bonded that their earnings out of commercial sex go towards repayment of debt. This makes them more vulnerable and beholden to the traffickers.

Child Prostitution

Further in countries like Netherlands, child prostitution has increased dramatically since 1990s. Similarly, in Australia child prostitution has increased sharply in Victoria as compared to other states, where prostitution has not been legalized. A study carried out by Christ Church School of Medicine, New Zealand revealed that nearly 2000 Christ Church prostitutes were under the age of 12. Girls as young as 12 years have been picked up by the police[8].

Some of the female activists and organisations working for the economic and human rights of the prostitutes would like to call prostitution a profession and argue that women have the right to choose the profession of their liking. However, prostitution is not a profession selected among other options by today's career women. Large numbers of street workers are homeless and live below the poverty line. Even women, who work in call or escort services have no control over the income because they are at the mercy of the pimps. Many complete their innings in profession without any savings.

A disturbing fact is that the average age of entry into prostitution in many developed and developing countries is coming down. In India, action research by the Institute of Social Sciences in collaboration with National Human Rights Commission revealed that majority of the victims were children. Children are preferred because of the clients' fear of contracting sexually-transmitted diseases. The hard reality is that the overwhelming majority of the prostitutes are not there by choice, but due to destitution, deprivation, ostracism, deception, etc. Many have been the victims of sexual violence either at home or at street, and many have been purchased from their starving parents by the pimps. Even before they reach their puberty, some of them are administered steroids to make malnourished children artificially plumpy just as cattle are fattened to yield more milk. The question of free choice just does not arise. Further, there is now greater demand for trafficked women and children because in many western countries, there is shortage of white prostitutes. In US for example, 70% of the prostitutes are non-white.

In Germany, lawmakers thought that they would be able to amass huge tax revenue when they legalized prostitution in 2002. But because of the criminal nature of the profession many of the brothel owners and the staff did not pay off and it was estimated by the Federal officers that the government has lost over 2 billions Euro a year from the unpaid tax revenue from the sex industry. Again in countries like Germany, Netherlands and Australia, normalization of prostitution has not occurred following legalization. Free women have not signed up for benefits or for unions. The reason lies in the basic fact that prostitution is not like any other job. Women are mostly engaged in prostitution, when they are forced to or have no other options. Even where, prostitution is legal, a significant number of women are being trafficked. Women and children, under the control of mafia and criminals are in no position to register themselves to authorities or join a union. Again, many women join prostitution as a temporary means of making money and hope that as soon as the debt is paid off and a certain amount of money is saved for the poverty stricken families, they will go home. They seldom tell the friends and relatives what they are doing to earn money. They naturally do not want to register with the authority and create a permanent record of being a prostitute. Unionism of sex workers is indeed very often incompatible with the coercive and abusive nature of prostitution.

Further, commercial sexual exploitation has another demeaning aspect. It teaches men that female bodies can be traded, used and discarded. It aggravates gender inequality in all areas of society and encourages sexual violence and harassment in domestic life as well as in work place. Indeed, prostitution is an insult to self-respect of women and violates their basic human rights. In a joint study on sex trafficking done by Coalition Against Trafficking in women and children funded by Ford Foundation, most of the 146 women interviewed strongly stated that prostitution should not be legalized and warned that legalization would aggravate risks and harm for women from already violent pimps and customers.

In 1999, Sweden passed a law, which makes a criminal offence for any person, who seeks casual sexual favour in exchange of payment. A law levelled equally at both client and the seller along with evenhanded enforcement would be a better solution than decriminalization. It is callous on the part of the government to abdicate its responsibility to provide decent livelihood option for women and children and pull them out of the inferno of prostitution. Instead of legalizing prostitution, the state should take steps to create alternative livelihood options for women and sex workers and punish those, who seek to exploit women with the intent of financial gain. Very often, under the laws of most of the countries, the prostitute is penalized and the male client goes scot-free. In India, under the Prevention of Immoral Traffic Act, there are provisions of punishment of traffickers, brothel owners as well as the clients but seldom they are visited with any kind of punishment. Only victims are re-victimized. This is unfair and iniquitous. Instead of cashing in on the economic benefits of sex industry by taxing it, government should step forward to provide to prostituted women economic resources from seizures of the assets of the traffickers, brothels-keepers and other captains of the sex industry.

References

1. Dr. Syeeda Hameed, "*Silence Around the Sex Work: Women's Future Service*" in http://southasia.onworld.net/article/view/123869/1/70.
2. Louie, R (1998), Project Client Call, Melbourne Macfarlane Burnett Centre for Medical Research.
3. Sullivan Mary, (2003), Making Sex Work in Victoria, PhD. Thesis, Department of Political Science, University of Melbourne.
4. Barclay, Ingrid, (2001), Interactive Process in Brothel Prostitution, Honours Thesis, University of Melbourne.
5. Voice of the Voiceless, Newsletter of NATSAP, Vol. 2, February 2006, Issue 2.
6. Murphy Padraic, (2002), Licensed brothels call for blitz on illegal sex shops, The Age, 3 June.
7. Voice of the Voiceless, Newsletter.
8. *Ibid.*

Index

J

K

L

V